GRE

41999

799.1755

E

D0119805

LONDON BOROUGH OF GREEN

SI   3 AUG 1976

D

799.1755

Stn

GREENWICH LIBRARIES

3 8028 00909673 3

A GAME FISHER'S
DAYS AND WAYS

By the same author

A Fisherman's Notes to his Son
A Fisherman's Recollections

A Game Fisher's Days and Ways

Norman Hill

Adam and Charles Black
London

First published 1976
by A & C Black Ltd
35 Bedford Row, London WC1R 4JH

ISBN 0 7136 1657 1

© 1976 Norman Hill

All rights reserved. No part of this
publication may be reproduced, stored
in a retrieval system, or transmitted in
any form or by any means, electronic,
mechanical, photocopying, recording
or otherwise, without the prior
permission of A & C Black Ltd.

Printed in Great Britain
by Billing & Sons Limited
Guildford and London

41999
799.
1755

Contents

List of Illustrations

To all those
splendid people
my
fishing friends

Foreword

Since the days of Izaak Walton and Charles Cotton a steady development has taken place in fishing tackle and the techniques employed in its use. In the nineteenth century split-cane rods and multiplying reels were established, and free-running Nottingham reels, and the first fixed spool reel, the Malloch, made long-distance casting possible for the average angler. Forward-tapered lines, agate rings and a host of other inventions appeared. In the twentieth century angling has been made much easier by the invention of beautifully light and strong hollow fibre glass rods, sophisticated lines, monofilament and efficient and easily operated reels.

In short, the mechanical side of game fishing has become more efficient, far less tiring, and consequently more enjoyable.

The writer of this record of a long and interesting sporting life has been fortunate in two ways. Firstly, he has lived through this latter period of enormous development in the products available to improve the enjoyment and effectiveness of angling. Secondly, he has been ever in the forefront of using and adapting these advances which, coupled with an exceptional skill in the art, have made him one of the leading anglers in the country for over half a century.

During the Second World War, he wrote two books, *A Fisherman's Notes to his Son* and *A Fisherman's Recollections*, and of these another eminent angler, Richard Walker, wrote '. . . so when I read your book again at the weekend, your comments had a completely new significance to me. This is only one of many instances where it transpires that Norman Hill had it all sewn up long before my friends and I ever thought of some of the ideas that are now used successfully. . .'

Much earlier, in 1924, following a visit to the United States he brought back some of the earlier plug baits, being convinced that they would prove effective in our native waters, and you will read of the success achieved particularly in salmon fishing.

Primarily a game fisherman, Norman Hill is by no means bigoted in his outlook, and turned his attention to salt-water angling during a short spell of residence in Southern Ireland, where he enjoyed some of the superb bass fishing that is offered in the inshore waters of that country.

You will enjoy his reminiscences and quickly realise that, despite his seventy years, he is right up to date and offers to the discerning reader a wealth of knowledge based on his long experience.

DAVID HILL

Introduction

AN AUTHOR embarking on the adventure of writing a fishing book must ask himself what prompts him to do so. Is it the vanity of seeing his ideas and memories on record, and in the hands of a public seemingly always anxious to buy any book dealing with its favourite sport? Is it for money? Is it from a genuine desire to help his fellow anglers to enjoy their sport more, or, put in another way, to enjoy more sport? Is it to fill in the long days of winter by recalling and recording seasons gone by, and already attracting to themselves that delightful halo of glory which invests things gone but not forgotten?—things which assume greater splendour as the years roll on. Fish that grow larger. Rivers at the perfect height for salmon to run. Clean healthy spring fish. Fine bracing days of broken cloud with sufficient sunshine, and only occasional showers. Ah, what golden dreams!

It is difficult to answer these questions with complete honesty. A little of each, in all probability, except for the financial part. There was certainly no money to be made from this labour of love in the past. Friends who wrote good fishing books years ago were discouraged by small sales and negligible royalties. Since their deaths we have seen a tremendous upsurge in the popularity of angling and its attendant crafts, such as fly dressing, with the result that some of their books are now best-sellers, being reprinted almost every year. Alas, it is too late for the authors to enjoy the fruits of their labours.

There are plenty of good fishing books but not so many great ones. The Waltons, Edward Greys, J. W. Hills, Skues, Plunket-Greenes, and Sheringhams do not come every day. If an author can attain even moderate acclaim he is doing well in view of the intense competition which has appeared in recent years. Perhaps the publication of new books has fallen off a little since 1971 but prior to that time they were pouring off the printing presses at such a rate as to be positively alarming. Many dealt more with the gymnastics of angling than with the spirit of it, and the charm of its surroundings. Illustrations of would-be Olympic gold medallists performing the most amazing and exhausting contortions, the sole purpose of which seemed to be to present a team of flies, no matter how indelicately, to the fish that are always that little bit out of reach; the nearby shore and weed-bed feeders being nearly decapitated by their efforts.

For fifty-five years I have fished. Lots of fish have come my way from hard-fished public and association waters, but I have been lucky in my friends and their kindness and generosity has made up for the lack of fishing of any real quality to which I should otherwise have been condemned, due to my comparative poverty. One needs very goods friends indeed if the best of English and Welsh fishing—the Wye, Teme, those few choice parts of the Severn, Welsh Dee, and their tributaries—are to become available. To say nothing of the Itchen, occasional days on the Test, and many private lakes and brooks in the Welsh borderland. Do not run away with the idea that all is friendship and brotherly love in the fishing world. As in other walks of life there are those who cannot tolerate your small successes, but that is the way of the world, and this book is aimed at bringing joy and a little instruction and amusement to its readers.

The sea-fishing chapters result from a holiday in Ireland in 1963. We were late in the season and sport was moderate, until we went to the coast and struck it just right for a large run of bass. I was so impressed that I sought out and bought a house of sorts within a few hundred yards of the sea. For five years my wife and I lived there and I describe some of the extraordinary sport on a light rod and line which can be obtained from this grand sporting fish. How different the present world is from those days. So few years ago! (In Ludlow market today the going price for mackerel, herrings, kippers and other such delicious, but universally recognised 'cheap fish' is about 25p each. Cod is over 50p a lb. On this reckoning salmon should be £5 a lb or more, and yet the market was full of them last season at 75p a lb.) At that time mackerel could be caught until one tired of it. We always gave them away, for a market price simply did not exist. Nobody would have given ten shillings for five hundred mackerel. On several occasions I left a heap of good cod on the little quay, beautiful fish of from 5 to 16 lb apiece, but nobody ever picked one up and took it home, although it was clearly understood that all were welcome to have them. Bass were the only fish for which there was any demand from locals and fish merchants alike, and with sufficient reason. They are delicious fish.

The market is odd and unbalanced when one considers the price of salmon in conjunction with Greenland netting, U.D.N., and our own disgraceful level of inshore netting. The obvious cause of this glut was a season lacking rain. Estuaries full of three- and four-year-old fish, so full in fact that in places they could be scooped out with a hand net, and hordes of predatory netsmen slaughtering right and left—quite legally—because of our anti-quated laws and ideas of a 'fair deal' for the poor netsman. The angler contributes vast sums to the upkeep and preservation of the breeding rivers, and the netsman pays the price of a round of drinks for a licence to make, literally, hundreds of pounds. No action of a satisfactory nature is taken and the scandal goes on year after year. The Wye is one of the only rivers with proper control of its estuarial affairs, and if it can be done on the Wye it can be done on every other river, and all can try to pay off or pension their few hereditary netsmen, ban the spare-time towns-man netter whose sole interest is money—tax free at that—and ensure that there are good and frequent runs of fish entering our rivers to provide the man who pays the high rents and rates, and all the other large bills, with the sport to which he is entitled. Angling is a sport for everyone—it provides needed refreshment for the city dweller as well as the countryman—and its delights are no longer limited to the fortunate few. This is as it should be, but unless some measure of control is introduced to restrict wholesale exploitation the future is grim indeed. Our beloved rods, reels and flies will gather dust in the attics, to become col-lector's pieces in the antique auctions of the future.

Advancing years do not bring many joys of a physical nature, but the mental processes calm down a little and the edge of keenness is somewhat blunted. A happy day is still possible although the bag may not be large. No longer must a fine heap of trout lie beside the angler as he takes his lunch, nor are two or three salmon necessary before the digestive juices can function properly. A morning salmon helps a lot, the grass is greener and the bird song is sweeter, but one is more prepared to accept disappointment, and a blank day no longer casts a gloom. More permanent in the memory than the fish we catch are the pictures of the river itself, running here over golden shallows, and there cutting darkly through steep banks, under overhanging trees. The haunts of delightful residents; the dippers, kingfishers, and wagtails that give charm and colour to the scene.

Lake fishing for trout is in a healthier state than it has ever been before, albeit of an artificial nature supported by large numbers of 'put and take' stock fish. It is a matter of opinion, but for me, no matter how attractive the lake may be, it cannot compare in variety of scene and water with the stream and brook. There is no alternative, however, if the ever-growing army of trout-fishers is to have sport. The rivers, streams and brooks are already fully occupied, and there are other dire problems of pollution and abstraction contributing to the shortage. In the lakes, any trout shortage can be regulated by increasing the numbers of trout farms for re-stocking them.

The salmon problem is vastly more complex. A migratory fish gains an almost unbelievable increase in weight in a short period of sea feeding, but the perils it faces are tremendous. If it survives its natural predators every man's hand is against it, from factory trawlers to stopping nets. Experiments are being conducted to raise salmon, like trout, to a sporting size in protected conditions. It is rather difficult to imagine a successful outcome in our present state of knowledge, but it would be a great step forward if it could be achieved.

The future holds grave problems for anglers. We can only hope that man will gradually develop more commonsense in his dealings with nature and the ecology, and that our beloved sport will survive. But we must fight the polluter, the abstractor, the commercial poacher and the avaricious netsman, whether deep-sea or estuarial, with every means at our disposal, and we must support, with money, those who struggle and fight on our behalf.

Chapter 1

Salmon Fishing.
General remarks, and fishing the fly

I AM NOT writing for the wealthy man who can afford to buy the best fishing for sums which might, at the present time, run into hundreds of thousands of pounds, or to rent expensive beats on Scottish or Norwegian rivers and take the risk of losing his money when the period of his lease coincides with drought, flood, disease, or any other of the hazards which beset the angler. But rather for the man of average means who gets his fishing by association or club membership, hotel waters, or the kindness of his wealthier friends who invite him to fish their more peaceful rivers. Even these modest approaches to the sport require the expenditure of fair amounts of money. Rentals, licences, ghillies and their tips, and all the other incidental expenses are quite substantial. We are very far removed from the days when, as Jack Hughes-Parry once told me, he fished some twenty miles of the best water on the Welsh Dee for a fiver a year. At about the same period my old friend Herbert Hatton of Hereford had the same story to tell. Miles of quite fair water, with rather more than a good chance of catching a fish or two, for very little money. That is all a far cry away. Today money is a 'must' if you are to engage in the sport at all.

The outlook for salmon fishing has become increasingly gloomy. Greenland netting, years of low water combined with abstraction and excessive estuarial netting. A disease which has defied all the scientific bodies, and a vast increase in the number of anglers operating almost by day and night.

Yet, miraculously, the occasional good year crops up and gives us fresh hope. In 1972, near to the division which H. A. Gilbert in his splendid book defines as the division between the Welsh and the English Wye, there was sufficient water to allow the excellent runs of fish which entered the estuary to travel well upstream and provide first-class sport on the minnow in the early period, and to the fly and plug later on. All this despite outbreaks of disease throughout the season, and here and there one or two pollution scares.

The year 1973 could have been another excellent year and it started full of hope, but the river fell away, fresh water only came in small spates at the wrong time, and the disease was of terrifying persistence all through the year, the bed of the river being paved with large dead fish. Other rivers had similar problems. Many of them, after an encouraging start, fell more or less into the same pattern.

You can inoculate your chickens against fowl pest, but wild fish cannot be similarly treated, and it is hard to see any effective remedy to U.D.N. other than the old one of nature building up its own form of immunity.

It is really remarkable that the fish are surviving in sufficient numbers to provide these occasional good years, and reassuring and encouraging to those of us who thought the salmon was facing extinction. Thank goodness they appear to have some secret feeding grounds that have not yet been located by man, with all his beastly detectors and electronic aids.

Even the much-fished rivers in easy reach of industrial centres, such as my local Severn and Teme, had excellent catches in 1972 and it is to these rivers, and their like, that the man of modest means must turn. They are hard fished, and the Severn in particular is not a river that clears very quickly; it can be out of fishing order for long periods during heavy rain. But they provide good cheap sport here and there. Likewise many areas and water systems in the west, north-west and north have similar facilities for the man of modest purse. On occasions I have had three and four fish in a day from the Teme, and on one never-to-be-forgotten day the Severn gave me the only bag of salmon I have ever had to remove in a wheelbarrow. Six fish of 23, 22, 22, 16, 13 and 9 lb in four hours fishing with an old yellow and brown minnow.

There is not the same feeling of privacy and opportunity in fishing behind other rods on a semi-public water, but it can be productive, and it is a good if stern tutor, making the angler, if he is to succeed, persist to the end of the day in spite of frustrations and annoyances. It also provides the competitive urge which is so essential, especially if you are, as I am, inclined to be easily satisfied and content to call it a day after modest success. There is nothing like the sight of another fisherman, humping a couple of fish along the bank, to stir you into activity and get you back into the river instead of sitting rejoicing over your one fish. That, of course, gives me the opportunity to emphasise the fact, so well-known to experienced fishermen but not always to amateurs, that salmon often come 'on the take' for only short periods, and it is more probable that you will get another one immediately following your first, than half-an-hour later.

How the angler obtains his salmon fishing is his own affair and obviously depends upon the amount of money available, but I would rather take my chance on water where fishing is available on any day when the river is in order, than have access to better and more productive water available only on certain days, or certain weeks. Salmon fishing is so dependent on water level that a one-day-a-week man might go the whole season without striking it right. Likewise the renting of an expensive beat far away, for the odd week or so, can, and very often does, result in bitter disappointment.

Good books written by sound and experienced authors are good friends and will give the modern angler many useful pointers. To mention but a few, such books as A. H. Claytor's *Letters to a Salmon Fisher's Sons*, *Fishing for Salmon* by Cyril D. Marson, *The Floating Line for Salmon and Sea-trout* by Anthony Crossley, *Rod Fishing for Salmon on the Wye* by J. Arthur Hutton, and my favourite of all, *The Tale of a Wye Fisherman* by H. A. Gilbert, are well worth absorbing. Great changes have taken place in tackle, transport and costs since these books were written, but not in the salmon themselves. As the good lady who tied my flies so splendidly for over thirty years—May Rudge—used to say to me, 'Remember, the salmon is still the same strong fish he always was'. That was to drag me back to sanity when I had become caught up with some new, ultra-light tackle craze.

The wisdom and advice given in those books is as sound as it was in the days when they were written, although, in some cases, quite opposing views were expressed and had their followers. An instance that comes quickly to mind is the insistence by that most superb of fishermen, Robert Pashley, that his pools should be absolutely rested, and even guarded against a shadow thrown on the river by an unwary pedestrian.

This teaching—very nice if you can preserve such solitude in these days—contradicts the school of fishers who think that occasionally it pays to have some disturbance, as salmon need waking from the periods of lethargy into which they fall. This is one of the strange contradictions that somehow make sense. To be the first down an unfished pool can bring excellent results. It seems to be due to the peace and quiet of the pool that a fish rises and takes your fly. But what do you say when your friend comes along behind you and takes another on his fly, after your fish has been fighting hard all over the pool?

And how do you account for an incident which befell me after fishing a well-known pool on the Welsh Dee blank, I fell in at the top, spluttered and floundered right through the pool, and came out in a sorry condition seventy yards downstream, only to return from the nearby farm, dry and changed, and proceed to catch a 22 lb and a 16 lb fish on the same water? I well remember discussing the incident with friends the same evening and listening to a variety of theories. 'The fish had just run into the pool whilst you were changing', was one of them. Fish had not been moving up for a week or more, although it must be admitted that the odd one creeps up from pool to pool in even the lowest and most settled water. Perhaps it is just another version of the old idea of 'Stoning the pool' or 'Putting a dog through it'.

Salmon fishing is full of these contradictions. If I were asked to name the greatest fault from which so many of us suffer I should say without hesitation, 'Not fishing out one's cast, whether with fly or bait', for I firmly believe that quite as many followers, and probable takers, have the fly or bait removed from their vision just as they are about to take, as those which take in the earlier stages of the cast and finish up on the bank.

I have watched this happen so many times when lying down

18

to observe the progress of a friend's fly, on those days when the light was just right for Polaroids to remove all traces of glare. Fish after fish has followed, nosing the fly or bait so gently that the angler has been completely unaware of anything at all happening, and has expressed astonishment when I have told him of the followers from whom he has snatched his fly just before the moment of decision.

Conversely, numbers of anglers argue that your fly is better engaged in the 'taking places' and it is time wasted fishing it right out in the slower stream, or perhaps, even in the backwater.

This has not been my experience. Many of my largest fish have followed half-way across the river to take in the uninteresting quiet water at my feet, or at the side of the boat. I grant that such fish are difficult to hook, and various stratagems have to be employed which shall be discussed later, but it is a choice of working the fly as far as ever possible to induce a take, or flicking it away and missing a chance which, whilst not visible to the angler, is there nevertheless.

It is really surprising how many ill-conceived things have been introduced into the equipment used by a salmon angler. One might almost ask some manufacturers, 'Who's side are you on, the salmon's or the fisherman's?' Just a few can be listed; there are many more. What about gaffs shod with metal, which clank whenever the angler moves across the stones? What of the flash clothing and white hats one sees worn on shallow stretches of good taking streams? Shining, gleaming rods, the flash from which can strike the eyes from afar? Finally, and worst of all things, the brightly polished steel gaff head or aluminium shaft which alarms the tiring salmon into fresh life and renewed vigour? A long list of angling stupidities could be drawn up.

Quiet clothes, rubber-shod gaffs with darkened heads on hazel shafts that will float but will not flash. Great caution and stealth when casting over a nearby lie, from bank or boat, dull rods, and of prime importance, a quiet angler keeping down low on bank or in boat when the fish is being drawn to the waiting gaff.

After money, luck would seem to be the next essential in salmon fishing. One must cultivate it with great care. It is a very real and dominating feature of an angler's life. A bit of luck is necessary in all of life's activities; business, profession, motoring, shooting, water sports, and, of course, gambling, but I personally have been more aware of the freaks of fortune in the realms of fishing than in any other occupation or pastime. This was borne in on me on a mild morning last March when the river was in good order and fish were showing in the lies. For some reason or other I decided to use an old spinning rod of 9 ft in spliced Greenheart, made for me by Herbert Hatton forty years before. It had been hanging in my gun room with my other numerous rods and it looked in good condition. I killed a 15 lb fish on it, and the rod gave a groan or two, which I attributed to the splice. I rebound the splice and went on using it. A fish took my minnow and when he first came out in a big surge I guessed him to be about 28 lb, not too miraculous for the Wye, but a good one. After some fifteen or twenty minutes of hard fighting, during which the rod was emitting the most alarming screams of agony, my ghillie gaffed neatly in front of the dorsal fin and swung a very beautiful $35\frac{1}{2}$ pounder into the boat. That gaff had landed hundreds of fish and although very thin in the metal had proved itself to be strong and trustworthy. All was well, and there was a slight tendency towards alcoholic celebration in the cottage when we returned. After lunch I went to another pool and at the second cast the rod literally disintegrated.

That was the first bit of luck in connection with that fish. The next was even more alarming. Later on a fish of moderate size, very active, and I think in the 17 lb region, eventually lay on her side and was gaffed. When the ghillie lifted, he sat down with an undignified thump in the bottom of the boat and my reel screamed as it released fifty yards of line in a great hurry. The metal of the gaff had snapped at the binding, where age and water had done their work. It was quite an affair landing that fish without a gaff, but it was eventually accomplished with the gaff head still in her, and the fact that the break had not happened when the big fish was being landed was the second bit of luck. Can you imagine what *might* have happened? A 35 lb fish played on a multiplier attached to a broken butt. Then, by a miracle, brought to the side of the boat where the gaff broke in the lift. What a nightmare thought!

My generous host insisted on my taking the fish home, and to round off the story my sister 'phoned to request a large piece of middle cut from the best salmon I could catch, quite sure that the usual excuse would be forthcoming, because she˙was running up to a twenty-fifth wedding party. It just showed that my luck held out to the end.

Fortune smiles upon you on those days when you throw your fly or minnow across overhanging boughs and a careful draw releases it time after time, and when the otter you always carry releases your minnow from grasping underwater lies and rocks, sometimes a dozen times in a day.

Luck. Yes! A very necessary ally for an angler to seek. Follow your hunches. When you feel that things will turn out all right, they often do!

It can go the other way, of course. A dear friend some years ago had a bad patch and lost fourteen fish on the trot. Broken rod, seized-up reel, weak line, frayed cast and even a swivel that pulled apart. My worst calamity was to lose a fish in the over 40 lb class at the gaff after four hours' play. It does not all go one way, but keep hoping. I even met a lady in Ireland who killed a 40 pounder on her first day of salmon fishing, after being given a black cat!

In conditions of clear bright water risk your luck by fishing fine. Salmon are not as stupid as some anglers make out. Fish will not tolerate thick nylon, heavy leads and large lures in such conditions. Come down to really sound trout tackle. It makes all the difference. Only yesterday I landed two fish of 25 and 20 lb on very light gear. One took forty-five and the other thirty-five minutes, but they had refused anything heavier, and so it was all worth while.

Apart from luck, I believe that the mental approach to fishing is of the utmost importance. I well remember the remark of an old friend who was a good salmon and trout fisherman, and certainly knew what he was talking about. He was asked why so-and-so was such a successful fisherman and his reply summed up one of the secrets of success. He said, 'Because before every cast he convinces himself that he is going to catch a fish, and that helps him to do so.'

The most pleasant, and one of the most deadly ways of catching a salmon is with the fly. The fight of a strong well-rested fish on a light fly rod is sheer delight. Nothing in angling has changed more since I was a young man than the fly itself. Those of us who were brought up on Kelson, and even the works of less dogmatic writers, had it instilled into them that certain feathers were as essential to catching a fish as bullets are to shooting a bird. It was a beautiful form of self-deception. Boxes of perfectly tied flies in the full range of sizes were a joy to behold, and even today are collected and revered as are the works of great masters.

But it has been amply proven that we deluded ourselves more than the fish. Today's flies catch more fish because they ride, look and hook better than those old glories. What is more important, they are cheaper if bought, and practically a gift to the man who can do a bit of fly dressing, and shoots his own squirrels and other small game.

I have, of recent years, simplified my tube flies so much that I cannot understand why I didn't think of it years ago.

Let me give an example. Take a plastic tube, straight and hard, of the size required. You can cut a range of sizes to serve all needs. Now, by a very simple method convert it into a body, similar to one of my favourite flies—the Jock Scott. This usually involves you in building a body part-black and part-golden from silk or nylon or one of the newer body materials, and then ribbing it. It is rather difficult because nylon tube is not an easy base to work on. So why not paint your tube? Half and half; black and yellow or any other colours to suit your fancy. You can still rib it with a bit of gold thread, and then make a solid, indestructible job of it by coating with varnish, Durofix, or what you will.

All that remains to be done to finish it off as a very killing fly is to tie in a nice little fingerful of grey squirrel's tail hair at the head and then varnish that off. You can vary the weights to your liking by adding a bit of lead or lead wire to the body. Personally I prefer the livelier unleaded fly fished with a sink-tip line. A range of Mustad trebles in various sizes, and you have some very killing flies. What is more you do not lose the value of the fly as we once did, when you hit the hook on a stone behind you. You can make a wide range of sizes and colours in a few evenings' work, and I find they hook better than singles or doubles.

I still carry a few boxes filled with the dear old Thunder and Lightning, Yellow Torrish, Jock Scott, Silver Grey, Prawn fly, and many others. But they come along as old friends. I fish with the cheap tubes.

Grey squirrel is a splendid, showy yet natural-looking fur in the water and fish seem to accept it in all reasonable conditions of water and light. Black and yellow furs are good killers and a modest sum spent on dyes will soon provide you with a wide range of choice. Do not be too conservative in sticking to the standard flies—design and tie your own and you will find they are just as successful.

I have not heard Muddler minnows mentioned very much as salmon flies, but a few of them will always be useful. I find them good for salmon, and when the salmon are off, many a good trout, large chub and beautiful perch has taken them.

It is a constant source of wonder to me when I watch a salmon angler select and tie on his fly that he does not pay more attention to the points. I always use Mustad hooks and these usually come from the makers with well-sharpened points requiring no further attention. But we all use hooks more than once and very often the points have suffered from contact with rocks and stones, or, more happily, with the hard parts of a salmon's jaw.

It should be an unfailing part of the salmon angler's drill to examine his hook points frequently, touching them up with a very fine file, or small honing stone if necessary. If there is any doubt at all, throw the blunted hook away into the river and start with a new one.

We all learn our lessons the hard way during the years. 'I'll not bother to change my hook as we are going in within the next ten minutes'. That remark I have made, and heard many others make, to our cost. Nowadays, with a weight of experience and some awful memories behind me, I would rather give up fishing for the day than fail to change my hooks whenever any doubt exists.

For fly leaders my preference is for Racine Tortue Nacrita nylon. Many of my friends do not bother to taper their leaders and use nine or ten feet straight from the reel, but I prefer to have a tapered leader. Bind a neat small loop in the end of your reel line and join your leader to it by means of a loop or a half-blood knot. I usually leave the thick nylon joined to the loop and make any changes I want by parting the leader lower down.

It is essential, however, to watch that the loop bound on the end of the reel line does not become weakened.

For lines I now use plastic-coated forward-tapered floaters or sinkers in preference to the old silk, oil-dressed, lines. They are very well balanced and efficient and far less trouble to maintain. My only criticism of some of them (it all depends on the make) is the fact that the coils put into them by the drum of the reel are apt to stay no matter how you pull them out, and this can make 'shooting' difficult. The lines made by Scientific Anglers and Masterline do not give this coiling trouble. For the usual run of water, say, three- to ten-feet deep in reasonable spring temperatures, a weight-forward floater with sinking tip is excellent. For low water conditions a floater, and for the occasional very cold water fishing with fly, instead of the more usual and generally productive spinning bait, I use a weight-forward deep sinker. Be sure your line is heavy enough for all work, except perhaps, for low water conditions. As a guide, on my 13 ft rods I use a No. 9 or No. 10. I have nothing but praise for the lines supplied by Masterline and ABU, but these plastic-coated lines are thick, so use the longest leader you can cast with comfort, and three feet of the finest nylon you think safe for the point. I don't go below 10 lb B.S.

That bring us to fly rods, and here there is a wide choice with great differences in price. If you are determined to have Hardy's beautiful split-cane rods you are likely to part with a lot of money nowadays. If it does not run to that, I can thoroughly recommend good hollow glass-fibre. Some of mine are quite inexpensive, made by Rudge of Redditch, and do all I require. They are light and thoroughly efficient. What a difference from the rods we used in our early days! Very often we had Grant's Vibration rods from 12 ft to 15 ft, and delightful they were. But they were much more tiring to use all day than the modern rods, and not too kind to fine gut.

In fact, the good modern rod with a line that is heavy enough, and suits it, does the job of presenting the fly with hardly any effort at all by the angler. As in shooting and golf, easy does it. No forcing! These forward-tapered floaters flick across the pools on the Wye as easily and smoothly as you could wish—if you let the rod do the work.

I think it advisable to buy a new rod. A second-hand one is as risky as a second-hand car—and remember my earlier comments on luck! Perhaps you could make an exception if you knew for sure who had used it previously. If he was a gentle and considerate rod user it might be all right. You will note that I say 'rod user' and not simply 'caster'. A lot of damage can be done to a rod in ways other than casting. Have you ever groaned at the brutality meted out to a good rod by the ham-fisted individual who has his fly stuck up a tree, or wedged between two rocks?

Whatever you do, buy the very best you can afford. Rods, guns, clothes and all such personal things have to last and give the maximum of pleasure whilst doing it, and good stuff is a sound investment if you look after it well. I have Hardy rods and reels which are as good as new after forty years.

It is not a bad idea for the novice to have a few casting lessons from a good professional. You may have pools on your water which require casts other than the plain overhead, and it is satisfying to do your Switch casts or Spey's cleanly and efficiently. Be sure to learn how to cast really well over your left shoulder. Overcasting is a bad thing: always try to throw a line long enough to cover the lie, but not any longer. It is so much easier, generally speaking, to hook a fish twenty yards away, than thirty-five or forty. Fish the fly with confidence. Nowadays there seems to be a widespread opinion that spinning usually beats the fly. Remember Pashley's bag in 1926. 535 salmon: 401 on fly!— and many on the trout rod at that!

For the general run of British rivers the following fly rods and lines should cover most needs. I emphasise British rivers for obvious reasons connected with the size of the fish which may be expected, the force of the currents, and the need for appropriate strength in every part of the tackle employed. Heavier and more powerful equipment will be needed for Norwegian fishing, and indeed for some rivers of the U.S.A. and Canada.

Undoubtedly for all-round work on rivers such as the Wye, Welsh Dee, Usk, etc., a thirteen-footer with plenty of kick in it so that a No. 9 or No. 10 line will go out without effort, is a good combination for all types of work, whether deep fly, or semi-floating, according to the line used.

A 12 ft or 12 ft 6 in. hollow-glass rod is ideal if a lighter weight suits the physical requirements of the angler better. For boat fishing this length is perfect, and if you select the rod so that it will take the same weight of line as the thirteen-footer, it will simplify matters.

For sheer delight, when the smaller but very active summer fish arrive, I have found an 11 ft rod with a No. 7 line just about perfection. You will not be able to bully your fish with such an outfit, but they will tire themselves out if steady pressure is maintained. Once you have pulled in the small treble, you will not have any need to exert strong pressure. In fact you will probably kill your fish quicker by light but firm pressure throughout, than by laying-on with the heavier outfit. I have caught many fish up to 16 lb on the Hardy 9 ft Jet trout rod. No problem at all, although it takes a little longer to bring them to the gaff if the set of the current is at all difficult.

Robert Pashley, the Wye wizard, used single-handed trout rods with very light No. 1 silk lines. This was partly because he suffered from severe physical illness. Even for the fit man there is much pleasure in using this ultra-light tackle. It is very obvious that a boat is most advantageous in such cases, and that bank conditions need to be straightforward when using a trout rod, but it is surprising how quickly even a large fish can be subdued by correct handling. There is nothing very remarkable or clever about it providing your leader is strong and you handle your fish firmly, and pull him off balance. The trick is to find a nice easy bit of back-water into which you can lead a fish when it is getting cooked. It is half the battle. If there is no such place, as in one very fine pool I fish, and the stream is fast and powerful throughout, life does, indeed, get rather difficult. It is then essential to have a ghillie, or a dependable friend, to deal with the gaffing.

Pashley advocated bringing a tired fish into a muddy backwater, where in his wading days he stamped about and stirred up the mud so that the fish could be dragged into this opaque mixture and gaffed whilst it was confused. A very good idea and one which I have adopted on occasion. There are two difficulties as I see it: the first is to find the muddy backwater if your fishing happens to be in the higher reaches of a river where the bottom is usually of rock, and mud is a rarity, and the second is the possibility of the clouded surroundings concealing the fish's whereabouts, if it is allowed to sink rather deeply, making the gaffing a bit chancy.

The reels to suit rods are almost too numerous to list, but I will only use a reel with an exposed back plate such as the Hardy Perfect, upon which the finger can exert the most sensitive pressure during the fighting process when the fish runs. Without this rotating plate at the back the angler is dependent on pre-set pressures, or checks, which are very inferior in performance. Some modern reels have exposed flanges on the outside front of the drum. These are almost as good.

It would be difficult to prove that there is any really correct or incorrect way of fishing a fly. Many an angler has fished a pool down to his own satisfaction, casting lightly and well, leaving the fly to come round in the generally approved manner. Or, perhaps, mending line and letting the fly fish like a dead thing— in the A. H. E. Wood style. Again, he may be throwing a long sinking line downstream and allowing the fly to dangle. He gives up, rather disappointed, and stands in the water after the best fly water has been finished. He lets his fly dibble about on a few yards of line whilst he lights his pipe, and then confusion! It has happened! His pipe drops in the water and he struggles into playing position, feeling wildly for the handle of his reel. The fish, having securely hooked itself without any help at all from the fisherman, tears across stream as this upheaval takes place. I have seen this happen on more than one occasion.

It is also not unknown for a superb exponent of the art of casting to almost lose his reason and wonder if there is any justice in the world. He has tried for an hour or so to drill a little sense into a hopeless pupil—a ham-handed individual who could not tie a blood-knot or dress even the roughest kind of fly—and yet, whilst his line was round his legs and he had not the faintest idea where his fly was, this dull fellow had found himself attached to a salmon.

Nevertheless, there are certain rule-of-thumb ideas which have been evolved over the years, and which most of us obey as a general rule—although we vary our techniques as we think fit, as a gradual build-up of knowledge becomes stored in our memories. Let us examine a few of these.

It must be accepted that many of us get pleasure from throwing a fly well, whether or not it attracts a fish. There is considerable satisfaction in feeling that there is complete unison in our movements. The perfect lift of the rod and the pull of the line in the air behind. The forward motion with a slightly upwards thrust, the release of the shooting line at the correct instant, the raising of the rod butt to the horizontal so that the line may streak through the rings without resistance, and the sight of the fly landing where we had intended that it should. I do not believe that this aestheticism is exceptional. To a greater or lesser degree every angler must feel it, even those men to whom the killing of fish is all that matters, and those who do it for money.

But we must be practical because to achieve the pinnacle of satisfaction the errors and frustrations of bad casting, bungled gaffing and, worst of all, the losing of fish through our own carelessness must be avoided. And yet we all lose fish. No man can teach another how to avoid that calamity. He can only try to suggest ways of improving his proportion of kills.

Sound tackle is essential in the first place, and in the second, the care and maintenance of it. It cannot be denied that the finest quality is the most satisfying and the cheapest in the long run. Cleaning of rods, oiling of reels, and most essential of all, the constant examination and retying of nylon leaders and the loops on reel lines. The feeling of security is worth all the trouble taken. You cannot learn casting from a book half as well as you can by trial and error. Get down to the river and work at the task calmly. Annoyance will lead to the worst fault of all: forcing. If you seem to be inept and have difficulty in casting as well as the more experienced anglers around you it may be advisable to seek good professional tuition. As in golf, it is not wise to fall into errors of style or timing at the beginning, for they only become more difficult to eradicate.

The most general error into which many beginners fall is to allow the line to respond to the pull of gravity and fall behind. The overhead cast should be a smart flip of the rod backwards, but not on a horizontal plane. It should be backwards and upwards, allowing time for it to partly straighten and pull before the equally smart and decisive forward cast. This forward cast must also be in an upward direction, just as if you are aiming at a target some feet above the water. After the full action of the rod has been used, and the line has been released and is well on its way, the left hand holding the rod near the butt can be raised so that the line shoots through the rings, which are now in a horizontal plane, with but little resistence.

All casting has been very much simplified by the beautiful well-balanced lines which are now obtainable. If possible buy them from a dealer who has facilities nearby allowing you to try out the line to make sure that it is heavy enough for your rod, and, if it is, your casting problems will be greatly helped. Most modern rods have the number of the most suitable line marked on them, but occasionally you will find that a size heavier will help, especially for short casting.

Even with a floating line it is unwise to lift, or attempt to lift a long length straight off the water. Draw enough back through the rings to ease the strain on the rod. The overhead cast is the general purpose one for most rivers. When you feel really confident that you can make a success of it you will find that you try many other casts and 'flips' that you could not really call by name: such as switch casts over your right, and then over your left shoulder, and you will be delighted to find how effortlessly and effectively they shoot out.

One of the best anglers with whom I fish can, and does, sometimes cast his fly a long way, but as a general rule he prefers a very short cast: only perhaps twelve or fifteen yards from the boat. Obviously these short casts are more effective when boat fishing than when one is confined to the bank, because the ghillie can put his rod into a favourable casting position—and don't forget that salmon frequently take a bait or fly 'on the turn'. You get a lot more turns per hour with short casts than with long ones. A little obvious perhaps, but it is surprising how many people overcast even when boat fishing.

No subject in fly-fishing evokes more dispute and discussion than hooking the fish. Whether it comes under the heading of setting the hook, tightening or striking, to no question is it more difficult to give the right answer. Only recently there has been correspondence in one of the leading monthly fishing journals.

The advocates of all and every differing method aired their views. 'Strike at once', say some. 'Give a little slack and then strike', say others. 'Give a lot of line and let him turn down', is the solution advocated by men of experience, and so on. A ghillie who had been in at the death of very many salmon summed the whole thing up most succinctly when he wrote words to the effect that 'they have either got hold of it properly, or they haven't'. That, very roughly, sums it up.

Nevertheless, in spite of these differing views I think one or two fairly safe rules have emerged. When fishing floating or sink-tip line with tube flies and small treble and the cast is made across and rather downstream, it is not difficult to detect the precise moment of the take either by the swirl of the fish, or the slight stopping, or run out, of the floating line.

Not very much of a pull is necessary to set these small trebles and it is more often right than wrong to tighten up almost immediately after these indications. It is, however, increasingly difficult to hook the fish as the fly comes round to a position below the angler. In fact, at the limit of the swing when the fish takes immediately below the boat, or groyne or wading position, it may pay to allow one–two–three, in terms of time, and a yard or two of line to go free, so that the fish can make its half-turn outwards or downwards, otherwise there is some danger of pulling the fly out of its mouth, even with the small treble. With the single hook the danger is even greater. When fishing with a fairly large single, or a double-hooked fly, I feel sure the delay in tightening can be longer. Wait to feel the pull. I never tighten from the reel. Hold the line to the rod for a firm hooking. But, of course, 'hands' matter!

Our weather and seasons can get so mixed up occasionally that summer conditions come in February and winter days occur in June. It is therefore unwise to lay down hard and fast rules by dividing methods into winter, spring, summer and autumn. Very often everything indicates a change to fly in April following a mild spell and rising temperatures, and only the following week we are back again to heavy cold water, golden sprats and large leads. Most of us will remember days in February when trout have been taking flies from the surface and salmon have seized the experimental No. 4 Thunder fished with floating line. On one such occasion on the Welsh Dee in mid-March a 14 lb fish took my No. 1 single hook Thunder in the air before it actually hit the water, and what is more, was well hooked.

It is wise, whatever the weather and water conditions on the day you propose to fish, to have a case in your car containing a full range of tackle to cover all eventualities. Should you be contemplating several days fishing, it is not only wise, it is essential, at all times of the year.

The most important single factor in fishing for salmon is the height of the water. There are certain ideal heights for every pool. It is wise to learn these, give or take a few inches or so, for that is the height at which you may expect your lure, whether fly or other bait, to be at its best and for the fish to take it.

I can name two pools within half a mile of each other where wide differences occur. The one, a pool of high repute, fishes best at an average height of 1 ft 10 in., but fish are killed when the gauge reads 10 in. and when it is up to 4 ft 6 in. The other is a low-water pool, practically impossible to fish properly over 1 ft 6 in. and its best height is 10 in.

Local variations and idiosyncracies have to be studied and learned, but one thing is sure. Once you know the pools on your beat and their best heights, the most deadly period of all is the beginning of a rise. The first inch or so is best and when the rise really gets going in a big way, that is to say 6 in. and more, it is, in my experience, all over, although some anglers do not agree.

Temperature is important only inasmuch as it influences the fish running. Indeed, one might say that the influence of temperature is significant in its effect on all life. Salmon will take in very low temperatures, but they are loath to run, and until the figure is over 40° it is hard to get in touch with them in any numbers if you are upstream. Once the water reaches 44° and above they will really run, sometimes like racehorses.

Two days before writing these words I caught two fish, each covered with sea lice, and we are one hundred miles from the sea. The water temperature was 49°.

Chapter 2

Spinning for Salmon

MODERN SPINNING is an attractive, artistic, and efficient way of catching fish. Very different from forty or so years ago when rods were built of greenheart or split-cane, often with steel centres, and they were usually longer and certainly a good deal heavier than the delightful split-cane and hollow fibre-glass in use today.

In those days reels were far less advanced too. It was as hard to become a good caster as it always has been to overcome the difficulties of golf. There was no such thing as 'instant fishing' as there is today, when a tyro can purchase a fixed-spool reel from a shop, fix it on to his rod, and without more ado cast a bait forty yards without giving overruns a thought. A fisherman was a skilled craftsman and the good old free-running walnut, or the light-weight Allcock's Ariel reel, with silk lines, really sorted out the men from the boys. Steady progress was being made, however, and the Hardy Silex and Westley-Richards' Rollo were fairly successful improvements.

The Illingsworth fixed spool reel was really the great breakthrough. This reel reduced the difficulties of casting to an acceptable level, and permitted the use of light lines for getting natural minnows and tiny artificials out a long way. I feel sure I have never owned a reel with a clutch to equal the felt and mica clutch of the No. 3 Illingsworth. It was the sweetest thing imaginable and why present-day makers have not used these materials, instead of the metal-to-hard-fibre clutches of today, is a mystery.

With new ideas and new materials manufacturers made steady

progress so that today there are so many splendid rods and reels for spinning that nobody, whatever their financial circumstances, need suffer as we did in the early days. If a man cannot become an efficient caster in a couple of days there is something very much wrong with him. I refer to the mechanical side of casting: there is much more to the fishing of a bait correctly than casting and retrieving.

But as we started the fly-fishing chapter with a brief reference to flies so should we commence with baits as the most important item in the spinner's equipment.

Don't save money on baits. They are vitally important and are relatively inexpensive. Before the salmon fisherman arrived at the very killing and simple wooden minnow of today a surprising and very complicated array of baits were developed since the turn of the century. Slotted metal Devons with a fearsome range of trebles bristling out of slits up each side and from the rear. Absolutely guaranteed to be bad hookers because just as the single hook or small treble is the best hooking arrangement for fly fishing, so is the single treble the best and most efficient for the spinning bait. On many occasions I have put this to the test and it has always been proved that three or more separate hooks make the setting of the hook almost impossible on minnow, prawn or spoon. If proof were needed about the inefficiency of multi-hook tackles I can supply it. To try out lures with two and three single hooks in tandem I resolved to fish them on a three-day visit to Blagdon in 1968, and, whatever failures I experienced, to stick it out without changing back to my more usual single hook. I fished Black Lures and landed seven fish from 2½ lb to 4 lb and when I bent down to unhook the fish and take them from the net, not one of the seven had a hook in it. Had steady pressure not been kept on, every one of those fish must have gone free.

The cheapest and most killing bait today is the wooden minnow. It is the easiest and most rock-and-snag-free of all baits and gets hung up less than the heavier metal ones. Colour can be painted on to suit all conditions, and if the otter fails to release a snagged bait the loss is fractional compared with others. I use them from 1½ in. to 4 in. and the larger sizes may be painted with a good gold paint, with perhaps a touch of red in it, instead of the gold sprat on a fan tackle which is much more expensive, and prone to breaking up during casting or when fished in turbulent rocky parts of the river. A golden sprat is an excellent bait on most rivers, but there is really very little point in making it more delicate and expensive than it need be. Neither have I found much truth in the old belief that soft-bodied baits are better hookers as fish hold them in their jaws longer. They don't get much chance to expel the harder bait if trebles are kept sharp, and anyway I contend that a hard bait slips through the jaws and the hooks dig in better. A fish grips a soft bait more firmly and this prevents penetration.

It is advisable to paint the smaller sizes of bait in dull colours to match the natural minnow, perhaps a quiet brown and black, and perhaps these will be useful in low clear water. For rivers at anything from correct fishing height to near-spate conditions, yellow-bellies are very nearly unbeatable. Many other contrasts are very showy and kill well. My favourites are black and ivory, red and gold, and blue and silver. By using a light lead a wooden minnnow can be held in front of a lie for as long as you like.

For the occasions when the river comes up in a dirty flood the metal bait has its uses. Especially good is the large 3 in. or 3½ in. aluminium Reflet. It gets down well on cold days of low water temperatures and literally smacks the fish on the nose when fished with a suitable Wye lead on the trace. There is more trouble with this bait getting hung up, but suitable conditions of coloured water mean that there is usually sufficient power in the flow to keep the bait working clear of the bottom. Anyway, no sensible salmon spinner ever moves an inch without his otter and his gaff.

Whilst minnows are under discussion it is a good moment to look at mounts and traces. Every angler has his own ideas. Years ago we made mounts of treble, red bead, Elasticum and a swivel, and the traces of Elasticum.

Today many anglers have adopted the simple method of threading the same nylon with which the reel is filled, through the minnow shell from head to tail, running on one of the red plastic tulips which fishing tackle shops supply, and adding a treble of appropriate size by means of a four-turn half blood-knot. I have now used this method for four seasons without any disasters. A trace, as we understood it in the old days, is no longer used.

When lead is necessary a Wye lead of anything from $\frac{1}{2}$ oz to $1\frac{1}{4}$ oz is let in to the line about 30 in. from the bait. If a lead is unnecessary, break in just the same and fix a ball-bearing swivel. Always use the four-turn half blood-knot. This arrangement is simple and strong and is free from that awful bugbear of the steel wire and Elasticum days—kinking.

The minnow will kill fish in most waters, but spoons, particularly the ABU Toby, and Mepps in various sizes and weights, are also great killers. The Mepps seems to have a fatal fascination for coarse fish as well as salmon and many a day I have had splendid catches of trout, pike, chub, perch and even grayling to add variety to the catch.

Other baits which are well worth carrying in your roll-over bait pouch are ABU, Krill, Salar, Glimmy and Koster.

Plugs! What killers they are. From the days when I returned from a visit to America in 1924 bringing with me samples of their short single-handed casting rods, Shakespeare multiplying reels and many strange contraptions designed to capture bass and pike I have had great sport with plugs.

Of the items of tackle I brought back I disliked the short casting rod and I still do. They may be useful for canoe fishing but they are not suitable for English fishing and have not taken on for anything other than some forms of boat spinning. In those days the multipliers did not have any automatic or centrifugal controls, and overruns were a nightmare. A little later on the Pfluger Supreme, Coxe, and the Elarex reel got over this difficulty and rose to new heights of simplicity for trouble-free casting. Their successor the ABU Ambassadeur is just about as perfect as a multiplying reel can be for casting, but it is still much more fun to play a fish on a single actioned reel. Unfortunately these are no use for casting light baits and plugs.

Of all the American developments there is nothing that provides more sport than the plug. In my opinion, based on the capture of a very considerable number of salmon on this bait alone, the Heddon River Runt in yellow colour is supreme for salmon. I do not regard it as a dirty-water bait, but for normal colour, and more especially for clear, low water conditions I find it is almost unbeatable. It is expensive to buy and cheap in the long run. It kills a lot of salmon, and if used correctly, without lead, rarely gets lost. My losses would not be above two a year.

Like all things, even mass-produced and seemingly identical objects vary in minute ways, and so it is with plugs. If you take half a dozen Runts it is possible that four will work vigorously and with throbbing energy, and the other two will not be so active. You have to buy them and take your chance. Unfortunately, the man behind the counter does not like undoing the elaborate plastic packs and allowing you to diddle them in a bath of water!

After the Heddon Runt which, if you wish, you can buy in various colours, I have found the ABU Hi-Lo to be good. This plug has an adjustable lip which permits it to be used to fish deep water. Again, it comes in various colours.

The market is full of plugs made in Hong Kong and other Eastern places. They look good, and are sold at a little over a quarter of the Heddon price. But, in my experience, only about one in half-a-dozen works well in the water! One plug looks very much like another, but it would seem that there is some little quality which makes for a good lively action; this is lacking in these cheap oriental copies. As in all things, go for quality. It is far cheaper in the end.

The consistency of the plugs' attraction is the thing which fascinates me. There are several places on the Dee and Wye where experience has given me great confidence in their use. I can think of half-a-dozen pools where a fish will come to the plug every time, always providing the pool holds a few fresh fish. And, even more valuable, is the way in which fish that cannot be rated as quite fresh will come for the plug. Methods of fishing baits and plugs will follow, but is it worth mentioning again and again that a good active plug, one that makes the rod top throb with action, is not limited to use in the conventional across and down manner. I have killed over fifty good fish on plugs thrown upstream past the lie of an active fish resting at the side of a ledge or boulder. On most occasions they are taken with a tremendous bang. Oddly enough, fish taking a plug fished across and slightly downstream frequently sip it in so gently that there is no break on the surface, although the plug is working only a few inches deep. Just like a wise old chalk stream trout sipping in a fly.

Plugging is a most fascinating branch of salmon fishing. One can travel light with nothing besides a light rod and multiplier loaded with about 12–15 lb b.s. line, a spare plug or two in your pocket, and the stock-in-trade without which you never move an inch: gaff; otter; priest, and carrier, and again—contrary to the experience of other anglers—I only remember losing one fish on a plug. I think colour matters a lot. Yellow is the great plug colour and accounts for most of the fish.

The prawn arouses much controversy in angling circles. Authoritative sources quote instances of fish being driven from pools by the use of prawn. I do not doubt this. At certain times and in certain conditions of water and light fish are very touchy and I can well believe that they take fright at many things.

I have caught fish on fly and minnow from a pool that has been prawned only just before. Again, that does not prove anything because these may have been new fish which have just come into the lie. But I have never seen this panic so often quoted. It is possible that the fish of the very gin-clear rivers of Scotland may be more sensitive than those in our rivers which may carry a bit more colour. Whatever the rights and wrongs of the matter are, the fact remains that sometimes the prawn is the only bait that will take the odd fish, and occasionally they will go mad for it. So, providing you are not infringing any rules, or displeasing your host, it is wise to be prepared.

Prawns are much better when they are fresh. Dried or preserved ones will do, but fresh ones are infinitely better. The tackle so often used is of the fan spinning type. It is important to see that the hook mount—a single treble has always proved a better hooker than a multi-hook tackle for me—is sufficiently long to enable the whiskers of the prawn to obscure the hook. The prawn is bound on very well with pink elasticated cotton and the bait is fished in much the same manner as the minnow.

How well I remember buying two spinning prawn tackles. The one outstanding merit they seemed to have were the hooks. They looked good and passed all the usual gentle tests of temper, sharpness, etc., that I always give them. It had been a long dry period of low water and nil catches and I particularly wanted a small fish to give away. An unexpected fish took, in the pool at the end of my garden, and when ready for gaffing the nice little

10-pounder gave a feeble kick—and departed. On examination, those three splendid looking hooks of the treble each had a very neat 'shepherds' crook' at the business end, and none of them could ever have penetrated the mouth of a fish. How to guard against such mishaps I do not know, short of testing almost to destruction.

This tender bait needs more care in the casting, but with the medium rod and reel there is no problem in this direction. Leads should be as light as possible so that the prawn can be dangled in front of the lie of a fish *for a long time*. I have seen a fish just below a bridge rush at a prawn as if it were just the thing it had been waiting for, after a dangle of nearly five minutes. Personally I prefer to be a bit slower tightening up on a fish which has taken a prawn, and fancy it gives a better chance if he goes down and turns with it.

A sink-and-draw tackle is preferred by many fishermen. It is just a matter of taste. Before the practice was prohibited by the Severn Authority a great number of salmon were taken by suspending a prawn very near to the river bed, on float tackle. It was such a deadly method that it had to be stopped.

It is a fact that fish will take a small prawn or shrimp cast out and left lying on the bottom, with a small treble threaded through it with a baiting needle, and I have had a number by free-lining without any lead other than a couple of shots. This, indeed, is a very killing method, especially with brown shrimps.

Fresh prawns are a natural bait, just as worms are, and fish will pick them up in the same way. If the angler keeps well out of sight it is remarkable how near a salmon will venture to take this fresh bait, but the slightest movement will put him off.

I think the use of any lines other than good monofilament is a complication, and totally unnecessary. Good pliable monofilament is magnificent material. Stick to the brand you have found to be dependable. I use Racine Tortue and it has never let me down yet. That is saying something when the mind dwells on the ghastly tragedies that occurred in the silk line days. You never knew when its strength would fail suddenly—usually at the worst possible moment!

Many great improvements and inventions have taken place in recent years in fishing tackle but the greatest of all is modern monofilament. For spinning lines and fly leaders it is superb, and when you use it on a hollow-glass light-weight rod you are enjoying two of the greatest benefits ever given to anglers.

Now, on our progress from bait to rod we come to the choice of reels and rods. The Ambassadeur multiplier is supreme in its class. With it, consistent casting of anything between thirty and sixty yards or more with perfect accuracy, is easy. Either the 6000C or 5000C are suitable for salmon fishing. For the past two seasons I have fished the 5000C and cannot wish for anything much better, but all multipliers leave room for improvement in the slipping clutch. It is difficult to attain the perfect adjustment. It can be a bit too light, in which case you are winding without effect, or a bit too tight and you get jagging. The principle governing fish control with all slipping clutches is obviously the American one of 'recover some line, and pump' but it would be much more pleasant to play the fish direct through a smooth clutch. Just recently the 6500 Ambassadeur has appeared. I am at present testing it, but undoubtedly the clutch is greatly improved.

For spring fishing with the spoon, heavy minnow, golden sprat or painted wooden baits and, say, 1 oz Wye leads, a Racine Tortue line of 18–24 lb is satisfactory, and the rod I use is a 9 ft. Hollow-glass rods are capable of withstanding rougher treatment when dealing with hung-up baits and general wear-and-tear, but when buying insist upon good screwlock reel fittings and stainless steel rings. Nylon will cut through soft rings in a short time. I have lined rings of various kinds on some rods, they add a little weight, and every ounce counts, but they do not wear.

For fishing the plug with a similar multiplier, or fixed spool reel, a rather lighter rod is required: 8 ft or 9 ft, but lighter throughout. It is in my opinion a great mistake to have a rod with a stiff action and a soft top. A butt action is much more pleasant to cast with, and play a fish on. You need a reasonably firm top to drive in the hooks, and remember that apart from the elasticity of the rod you have a considerable line stretch to overcome. The line should be about 12–15 lb b.s.

For the lightest summer fishing you may care to go down to a 7 ft hollow-glass rod and small fixed-spool reel or an ABU 505. Use the light Mepps spoons or small plugs, and when you hook a fish you may be in for a long fight. The pressure you can exert is small, and you kill the fish by annoying him into fighting and exhausting his strength, but the charm of this light outfit is its suitability for using small fresh shrimps, either red or brown, and these can be deadly in low water conditions. Also your Mepps will catch any number of trout and coarse fish, and if you can name anything better for breakfast than a nice trout and mushrooms, or fillet of Wye perch with the same trimmings I should like to hear of it.

The choice of a fixed-spool reel for fishing in medium conditions is wide. There are dozens of them. I have used many (some good, and others not so good) and I now use a Mitchell 300, a very good reel indeed. And that, I think, is the essential equipment which you should buy, not necessarily all at once, but as you progress from one type of fishing to the other.

I have mentioned the roll-over bag or pouch I use for carrying baits and other small items. This is a leather concertina-type of bag which is the greatest boon to anglers of any carrying device I have ever seen, and the extraordinary thing about it is that it appears to be unknown, simple as it is. I received one from an old friend and great angler who had, as far as I know, designed it, and had a few made for his friends. I used it for twenty years, until in a moment of excitement I left it on the river bank, full of minnows, spoons, swivels and other valuables. That one was made privately, and so I had to describe it to a leather-worker who produced an excellent copy, for about £2, which is still with me. I give a photograph of it as it is worth its weight in gold, and quite possibly, in these days of mad inflation, that is about what you will have to pay for yours. But it is worth every penny, whatever the cost, for it carries all you need far better than tin boxes which knock all the paint off the baits, or plastic boxes which crack at the first blow they receive. It will slip into your game pocket, or the side pocket of your shooting jacket. It is, in short, an item of joy which should be amongst every salmon angler's paraphernalia.

The best gaff is the old Wye pattern. Simply a good strong hazel stick about 4 ft 6 in. to 4 ft 9 in. long, according to the angler's height, with a really well forged lash-on gaff bound on. The gaff should taper all the way round the bend and be needle sharp. You will not get one from the tackle shop, but you might persuade your local blacksmith to make one. It will provide you with a dependable wading staff (you will need one on some rivers!) and float behind you when wading if you attach a sliding ring to your leather carrying thong. The best safety guard for the point is a champagne cork. You will lose this frequently, which is not a bad thing to do, as it provides you with a good, if expensive, excuse to replace it. Alternatively, a piece of plastic tube is quite as good.

There should be no half measures about the priest. This must be capable of knocking a fish out once and for all. There are not many situations more difficult than wading deep under a cliff, a position at which you have arrived after much tricky wading, and trying to land a fish without really being able to move with confidence. When the moment comes for gaffing and you have the fish evenly balanced on the gaff you are in trouble unless you can despatch it immediately. Once that is done there is no further danger of it getting off the gaff. Whilst all this is going on it is sometimes a good idea to push the butt of your rod down your trouser waders so that you have both hands free. In the awkward situation described, the carrying thong of the gaff can be used as a sliding noose and slipped over the fish's tail. It is then very simple to wade out to safety with the fish floating beside you.

The next essential for any salmon angler to carry, or to have in the boat with him, is an otter or bait releaser. In its simplest form any piece of heavy wood (weight is essential so that the otter gets a good bite into the water) with a piece of cord tied round the middle, and a loop some 9 in. from the wood. Through this loop a chicken leg-ring is attached. Simplicity itself, and yet it is comparatively rare to see an angler carrying one. In nine cases out of ten this device will release a hung-up bait, always providing the angler has not pulled the hooks in by laying on in the first place. Get above the point of hang-up. Let the chicken ring take the otter well down beyond it, and see-saw the line by hand—and not by the rod as is so frequently done—until you come free. About the only situation that is really hopeless is when the hooks are firmly embedded in wood.

Waders, whether trousers or thigh, are important. In fact your life can, and often does, depend on them. Most of us have tried the lot; felt soles, rubber, leather, studded and so on. I have never found the perfect grip for all bottoms yet, but I must say that I am very much impressed by the gripping qualities of Geoffrey Bucknall's Griplastic thigh boots with their metal fibres embedded in the sole. For trouser waders I know of nothing better, and easier to slip on and off, than the Breast-Hi. Get them large enough for extra thick stockings to be worn.

Finally, when you have taken your fish to the hut or cottage to be weighed and recorded give it a tidy-up, lay it out in a clean condition with its fins extended and the body in a nice curve. I find the display of a beautiful fish, whether in the back of your estate car or on the lawn, leaves a lasting impression in your mind to finish off a good day.

Chapter 3

Two Spring Days, and General Topics

THE WATER may be in fine order, clear, yet with that very faint greenish tinge which can be an indication of good things ahead. Warm air from the south or west and a sky which prevents the sun putting too much of a glare on the water. You fish fly, picking one which you consider to be reasonable in size and colour. You catch two fish, and as you lay them out in the back of your estate car so that they look neat and clean and ready for inspection, your eye falls on the reserve tackle, and you wonder why you have brought it.

On the next morning the wind has gone round to the north and it is dull and uninviting. You put on an extra pullover and drive over to the river. To your astonishment you find it up eighteen inches and a bad colour. There must have been quite a lot of rain up on the hills ten miles above, but it is starting to fall. It is none too warm and the water and air temperatures are both down. But as you look at the top lie, opposite the gauge, you see a fish show in that unmistakable forward surge of a runner. In the space of the next five minutes you see three more. Obviously they are moving up and the spinning tackle replaces the fly rod of the previous day. There are those who state that running fish cannot be caught. Many eminent authorities incline to that view. And yet, on the Wye, we sometimes think that the running periods are the only times when we do catch fish. On the rare occasions when a lot of fish are settled in the pools good sport is almost assured, always providing that they are fresh fish, and not stale old-timers that have been heavily bombarded downstream. But a very high percentage of the season's catch is made up of running fish. Fish that one sees first perhaps half-a-mile below, and which show several times on their way up your pool. They are by no means all caught in the recognised lies; many of them being taken on the 'wrong' side of the river, and from behind or beside stones which, at normal heights, are in water too shallow to hold fish.

In such conditions the yellow belly minnow, or the golden sprat imitation, from $2\frac{3}{4}$ in. to 4 in., seem to be the best baits. Running fish are not easy to catch. I well remember, in a season when fish were few and far between, seeing one jump when he entered a pool on the Welsh Dee. This was followed by a further showing as he progressed up the pool. This pool, Ty-Newydd, is perhaps the best part of ninety or a hundred yards long. I went on spinning from the narrow neck of the pool and just when I judged the fish must have arrived, my 3 in. Hardy yellow belly was taken with a tremendous bang, and after a few very hectic moments of screaming reel and rapidly disappearing line, the fish leapt from the water in exactly the same spot at which he first showed. After that wild run he was absolutely whacked and I worked him back upstream to the gaff. The odd thing about this incident was the fact that the minnow was so far down the fish that it was not only completely out of sight, but I could not even feel it when I poked my finger—and I have very long fingers— right down the gullet as far as I could. Like may other anglers I have debated the 'do salmon feed in fresh water' question many times, but had this been a natural, unattached, small fish that he swallowed, he could hardly have done other than pass it through his body. Incidentally, the top end of this pool was a good place for the River Runt plug. There is a lie at the top of it, but the fish never took the fly or plug there. They always followed it very quietly to within three inches of the nearside rocks, and then it was sucked in with a very gentle sip. That is one of the reasons why I am such a firm believer in fishing the bait right out until the last possible moment.

On fly, minnow, plug and prawn the angler gets mysterious little plucks and tiny pulls. Make no mistake about it, these are usually due to a salmon touching the bait. So often one remarks to the ghillie, 'A funny little touch' or 'An odd little feeling of drag, might have been a trout, or a perch, don't you think?' We all have these, and some anglers are more sensitive to them than others. But how often does it turn out that at the very next cast a salmon takes, and is firmly hooked.

By watching fish through Polaroid spectacles you realize that their reactions to baits and fly are quite unpredictable. It is well worth watching a channel beside the bank when your plug or fly gets to the very short line position. Always providing you are well camouflaged, or hidden behind a bush and you blend with the background, you will notice that some following fish do nothing at all about taking the bait. They may follow more than once with the same negative result. Others follow with their noses some two to six inches from the rear of the bait. Just occasionally one of these fish will bunt the bait— it looks quite a smart rap—but the holder of the rod will not notice more than the odd tremor or tiny pluck.

I have done quite a lot of experimenting with these short-coming fish but have not met with very much success based on the traditional idea of changing to something smaller. Occasionally I have succeeded by putting on a larger fly, but when fishing plug, a livelier worker has several times been the answer. On balance I think the same bait as before—the original—fishing along exactly the same track does the trick more often than not. Always providing it is a lively worker. Or a lightly dressed fly with lots of movement in its hackles or fur. It is a good idea to bring it over the fish faster on the second, and we hope final, presentation.

The subject of lies and taking places is a vast one and each and every river has such wide variations that anything like an attempt to generalize must be doomed to failure.

One thing is certain. A good ghillie who really knows his river at all heights and in all conditions is beyond price. The knowledge which flows forth from a fine ghillie's memory should be absorbed with gratitude, and great persuasiveness and discretion should be the order of the day. Many are very funny fellows, jealous of their knowledge, and impatient of fools who doubt their advice, so obey your instructions, show him that you are capable of carrying out his commands—and command is the operative word in many cases—and you will earn his respect and gain his confidence.

The man with the most fantastic knowledge of taking places, and also the most unerring wielder of a gaff I have ever known was a lock-keeper on the Severn, He really was quite uncanny. Neither did he defer to anybody, whether he be Judge, Knight, Admiral, Brigadier or anyone else of high social standing. All were treated the same. Many resented it, and that was the end of them. The door was closed, and they could go away and fish by themselves, usually with little success. He very soon sorted out his sheep. He would look you over and most likely open his remarks with something disconcerting such as, 'Hope you aren't one of those barmy b——s who think you know better than me. When I tell you to throw in a certain place, do it, and do it accurately, d'yer understand?' Charming! If you had any sense at all you responded with your most friendly, warm and reassuring smile, and if you survived the hostile scrutiny for a minute or so, you might with luck, be 'in'. But it was a real test of courage to earn his confidence and friendship. He must witness your ability as an accurate caster, a player of fish, a quiet boat-mate, and a lurid and robust cusser. He was quite unique.

When he took me out we commenced at 10.30 am. An angler who commenced earlier had already taken a good fish. Smith, for that was his name, stated that the river had risen ten inches overnight, was a good colour and fresh fish were in the taking places. 'But,' he added, giving me a meaning look, 'they'll only be caught by them as can fish.' We started out and I was instructed to cast my 2½ in. very tatty yellow-belly so that it fell just past a slight swirl in the water some twenty yards away.

I cast, and my minnow fell ten feet past the swirl, but in perfect line. Heavens above! Did the world shake as he poured invective upon me? 'What do you think this is—a b——g distance casting competition?' roared he!

I mended my ways very speedily and satisfied even his exacting requirements. His knowledge was perfection. 'There is one there' —and this in the murky waters of the Severn! 'Just in line with that stone on the bank and about ten feet out.' 'Not bad, try just a yard nearer to us.' Bang—into him! Away he goes and fights deep down and very powerfully for sixteen minutes. He tired a bit, but did not turn-up or show his side. Nowhere near ready for gaffing, I thought. But the fish made the fatal mistake of passing close to the boat, and that was it! Six feet of water above, and well beyond the keenest eyesight, one would have thought. Four feet of gaff shaft and two feet of arm went down in the water, almost to his shoulder, and twenty odd pounds of very surprised salmon was on the deck. I wanted to protest but was not man enough to face his eye. He knew exactly where every fish lay, or should have lain had it not been disturbed by another angler. To an inch! 'They would have been in different places yesterday, a yard or so away from where we got them today.' That was the degree of accuracy.

So it went on, one big fish after another, until six lay in the boat, and I feel quite sure that on my own I should have been lucky to land one, or at the most two.

This story is told to illustrate the degree of precise local knowledge of a pool that is required. What hope has an occasional visitor, or even the man who rents a beat for a few weeks? He has no option, in the absence of a supreme ghillie, but to fish the water, concentrating on places above and below rocks, or where streams converge, or features likely to indicate lies, occur. He may have a very good eye for water, but lies do not necessarily mean taking places. Taking places are often quite indistinguishable from the bank or boat. They are certainly not always the obvious places, and it is only long and careful study of the water in all heights that discloses their whereabouts. Then, when you have served your apprenticeship and fancy that you know some of these precious spots, up comes the river ten inches or so, and they are all different. It is indeed a puzzle.

It is wise, if you think of it at the time, to make a pencil note, to be transferred to your diary later, of every fish you catch. Time of day; position of sun; height and colour of water; temperature; size of lure, and as near as possible the exact place where the fish took. If you are fishing alone it is really the only way to gradually build up a picture in your mind of the taking places in each pool.

Fish love a feature of some kind to rest against, or shelter under. This does not suggest that taking places do not exist where, as far as the human eye and knowledge can ascertain, there are no outstanding features. Many waters as uninteresting as a canal are good taking spots year after year.

Such features as overhanging boughs of trees, willows growing actually in the river and throwing their shade-giving shoots over the water, and, oddly enough, fences that run down to and enter the water, are all places favoured by salmon. Many of them look terrifying spots to fish, but fortunately salmon have not the urge to dive into the roots when hooked, as would a trout or a chub.

If you arrive on a strange pool alone, with no possibility of a mentor to advise you, you have no option but to fish every likely spot on your way downstream. And then try backing-up from the bottom to the top, so that your fly or lure is presented in a different way. It very often works. If all this fails, try the unlikely spots. They might turn out to be better than the good-looking ones.

Another variety of action and appearance which may be imparted to your bait, is by changing the speed of presentation. The fly may be fished down without action being imparted at all. This is the most usual method. If it does not work, try a little give-and-take line pulling; a few inches in and a few out, by using the left hand. This will give your fly more life than the old idea of waggling the rod top.

Plug action can be varied tremendously, but as a matter of fact my plug successes have usually been when I was retrieving in a straightforward manner.

The minnow has supporters of the no reeling in method and letting the lead bump round, scraping the bottom all the time. Other anglers fish the minnow higher in the water and wind slowly and steadily, whilst a few believe in a series of 'fast, slow'. I think it largely depends on the water temperature. On days of cold air and water, the bottom bumpers have it. On average days in spring and early summer the slow straight 'off the bottom but not quite midwater' method has always been my favourite.

The playing of a fish requires some thought. The generally accepted method, recommended by word and picture, is to keep a rod top up. This may be absolutely correct inasmuch as you are providing the maximum spring and resilience by holding your rod in that position. But this is a method handed down from times when man had only crude tools at his disposal and his sporting, or rather hunting, weapons were of a very primitive

A fine Wye salmon pool

A fresh-run 35 lb Wye springer

The happy fisherman: the twelve-pounders are dwarfed by the giant angler

One of the few places on the trout brook where a long cast is possible

The Teme: the lower garden pool

Splaugh Buoy: a fast-running tide

The flat-bottomed 'cot' used for inshore fishing off the Irish coast

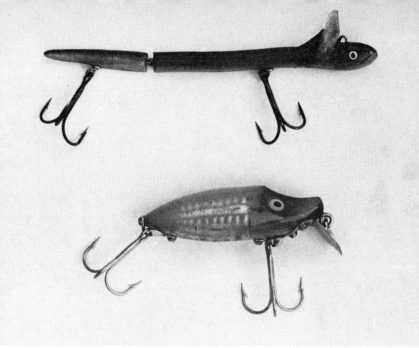

Two unbeatable baits: (*above*) the jointed plastic Sand Eel for bass, and (*below*) the Heddon River Runt which takes all predatory fish

The best way to carry baits: an expanding leather pouch

Perfect Wye spring fish: three of these a day should satisfy any angler

nature. It did not change much until the early twentieth century. Nowadays the picture is quite different. Rods are unbelievably tough and flexible, and lines are so strong that only accidental contact with sharp edges, or neglect on the part of the angler, is likely to break them, always providing that commonsense breaking strains are employed. Consequently a good deal more pressure in the way of side-strain, and other forms of dominating play, may be used with safety. Side-strain is the way to pull a fish off balance. Once he is off balance he can no longer lie in his normal position with his nose upstream and his gills working normally. A lowered rod exerting powerful side pull gets over that stalemate position in which we have all found ourselves at some time or other, i.e. a fish opposite your stance or boat, seemingly quite content to stay there for ever, and you exerting a constant pressure to no avail. Try to get below him, lower your rod, not to a direct pull, but to a powerful pull with it held at some 45–60°, and he should be thrown off balance and be very worried and start to fight—and it is a fight you want. A fighting fish does not last long; it is the stubborn fish that lies doggo that wears out your leader and eventually beats you. Whether you bank or boat fish, get below him and pull his head round. If you are stuck on a bit of bank above him you cannot follow this advice and other stratagems must be thought out. Perhaps a slack line will do the trick, or maybe you can walk him up to a position where the angle will be more in your favour. I have never found the much recommended banging on your rod butt to be of much use, but in desperate plights I have found that a well-aimed stone can be most helpful. The golden rule is to try to keep him on the move. Once he gets below you, in a powerful stream, you are in real trouble. A lot of backing, a friend downstream who will beat the water for you, or a most exceptionally powerful prayer are all I can suggest!

Eventually, it is hoped, the fish will be tired. His runs will become less powerful, and he will come nearer in. It sometimes seems to be an age before this happens. The fish will stay some ten or fifteen yards away from the gaff and it will be hard to move him closer if the current favours him. This is when silence is golden, and the angler should try to remain invisible—or as invisible as a fourteen- or fifteen-stone human being can make himself. Sit in the boat, as you should have been doing all the time you were casting—and make your ghillie do likewise. If you are bank fishing, either adopt Robert Pashley's excellent idea of muddying up a backwater, ready to confuse the fish and gaff him when he is at a disadvantage, or if that is not possible, get into fairly deep water and remain quite still. Fish shy away from shallow water, expecially when they realise that they are in danger, so if you can, keep three feet or more of water under your fish at this stage of the proceedings.

The actual gaffing can have problems and they vary according to the size of the fish. Generally speaking the larger the fish the easier the gaffing should be. Tire the fish out until he is wallowing about within reach of the gaff, but never on any account try to gaff prematurely. Then place the point of your gaff well across in front of the dorsal fin, lower it until you touch the fish lightly, pull it in, and then draw the gaff and fish towards you, lifting meanwhile. (You should not gaff under the fish, in the belly. A struggling fish can tear the gaff out of this soft flesh.) Do not hesitate at this stage. Straight into the boat and hit him with the priest, or right up on to the bank, run well back into the field, and use the priest before removing the gaff. Coolness is the keynote to good gaffing. Once you get flustered and miss the first time, you will probably start slashing at the fish in desperation, and the result is almost inevitable. Oh, the number of fish I have seen lost at the gaff! When everything should be smoothly carried out, some moment of panic so often comes to the rescue of the fish that has done so much to earn his freedom. Do not listen to the few anglers who have strange ideas about gaffing in the head. Until a few years ago I had never come across this particular peculiarity but, oddly enough, I have had this method brought before me on more than one occasion recently. The idea behind it is that the market price of fish is lowered by gaffing in the back. Very odd indeed when the fish are not to be sold! The whole thing is a fallacy. Any attempt to gaff in the head is asking for trouble. The head is hard and a gaff point can slip off easily, and the leader is within inches of the gaff head. Can anything be more certain to court disaster? Finally, the fish bleeds very badly and makes an awful mess in the boat and all the surrounding tackle bags, boat seats, etc. Should you prefer an unmarked fish, use a tailer. When fishing alone I feel safer with the gaff.

Small fish can be very difficult and dangerous to gaff. They are so active, and the target is small. Whenever conditions favour it try to walk a small one up the shingle, or net it. When you have to gaff, turn the gaff head round slightly to reduce the span of the gape, before gaffing. Some funny things happen when it comes to gaffing time. Dr Stanley Barnes, who wrote the book on *Knots in Gut and Nylon* would decide immediately after hooking where he was going to land a fish. He would then take up his stand, and nothing the fish could do would shift him from it. I never saw him lose one.

I believe in desperate measures when they are necessary to turn a fish out of trouble, and feel sure that more fish are lost by soft treatment than by showing who is master of the situation. In cases of reel failure or rod breakage, I have been known to hand-line a fish to the gaff. It is easier than you think.

Gaffing can be a great leveller; it can cut the pompous angler down to size very smartly. For many years I occasionally fished with a man who was an excellent fisherman and a good writer on some topics. He did not give any other angler much credit for possessing knowledge or ability to compare with his own. I once stood on the bank and watched him playing a good 25 pounder very well. Knowing him, I did not offer to gaff, but said quietly, 'I am here if you need me.' No reply—not even a nod! The water was not easy for gaffing. The rod was a 14 ft 6 in. Playfair and he was fishing a point fly and dropper. The fish was upstream of him, floundering about heavily and the stream was bringing him down to the gaff. He would have to be quick or the fish would be past him and carried away. He unshipped his gaff like lightning and just as the fateful moment arrived the fish sensed danger, swirled, and ran between his legs. Our wading equipment in those days comprised strong canvas body waders, outside woollen stockings, and heavy brogues. The dropper engaged the stockings and I expect you have guessed the rest. A broken leader, a lost fish, and a stricken rod with a top-joint pointing where it shouldn't have been! This terrible moment hushed me into silence. He then spoke. 'I would prefer that you did not remember that incident,' and his voice was sepulchral. I admit I did rather a lot of chuckling to myself as I fished the next pool.

I am a fanatic when it comes to sharp gaff points and in consequence suffered terribly at the hands of a fine old Wye ghillie. He was a splendid man in all ways but the point of his gaff had to be seen to be believed. It resembled the point of an ordinary ·22 bullet. It was as blunt as that! The first time he gaffed a fish for me it took three pokes before the gaff could be persuaded to go in—and I very nearly had three heart attacks in the meanwhile. I am not normally a discreet person, but I never dared to remark on that gaff, nor did my friend and host. Some things remain better unsaid!

Of course, salmon can be the most stupid creatures imaginable. This old ghillie told me some almost unbelievable stories of fish that disregarded all the rules. Fish that literally committed suicide. I can well understand how these strange happenings stuck in his mind.

A friend of mine had two experiences which I hope he will not mind me repeating. The first was a fish jumping into his boat, and the second was equally astonishing. He was trying out minnows to see which seemed correct for the colour of the water. He rejected two, and had just decided that the third was equally useless when a fish rose up, two feet from the boat, and took it firmly and was well hooked. So much for the angler's opinion!

Chapter 4

A Bitter-sweet Memory

On 28 September the Dee was in perfect order; the gauge showed 1 ft 3 in. of clear water, and the weather was everything a fisherman could desire. Fish were moving up and I had caught a few of moderate size, and some sea-trout, during the preceding days. The daily taking time seemed to be early, and I started down Lower Henfor at 9.30 am. Half-way down the pool a fish came up to my fly (a No. 3 Thunder and Lightning body only, with one bit of hackle and a fraction of wing) and refused it. I examined my gut cast and fly to find the reason. I found that the cast showed up very white in the clear water, so I hunted for something less conspicuous in my cast damper; it seemed to be a choice between a nicely tinted cast of 0·012 in. (very fine, but quite strong enough for 15 pounders) and nylon, which I did not trust at all. (See note on page 55). The 0·012 in. went on; the same tattered Thunder adorned its point, and at the tail of the pool it was taken, quietly and without any surface disturbance.

At first the fish felt like a 15 or 20 pounder; strong and active, but not in any way exceptional. Then he made a very fast run. The line went down and down towards the bottom of the deepest part of the pool: the whole of the dressed line and ten yards of backing disappeared in a flash, and with over fifty yards out, I was beginning to wonder what would happen next. Almost immediately afterwards an enormous fish practically beached himself at the top of the back-water on the enemy's side, and then I realised that I was, indeed, into the fish of a lifetime.

Our Hon. Secretary, who was present, caught a glimpse of

the fish's great tail and remarked, with his usual humour, 'His tail's like the rudder of the Queen Mary!'

At this stage everything looked fine; the fish was fighting well and working upstream, and my fine gut had withstood the first great shock. But almost immediately afterwards he changed his tactics and became dour; he hugged the bottom and sailed in a slow and ponderous manner round the pool for half an hour. Then he got really bored with the whole business—in spite of the pressure I was exerting with my 13 ft 6 in. Playfair rod—and settled down solidly some twenty yards out. I used side-strain, threw in stones, and did all the other things recommended for sluggish monsters, but to no avail, and there we stayed for another half-hour. Then a bit of extra side-strain upset him and he went (to my great relief) upstream. At the top of the pool he changed his mind suddenly, and in a flash went down the pool, straight through the tail, through the Upper Mount Run and into a convenient back-water some sixty yards down. I followed—very hastily—with nearly a hundred yards of line out, and got as near as I could to the place where he had taken up his new residence—some fifty yards beyond the limit of my wading and well over towards the opposite bank and, for the best part of the next *three hours*, that is where we stayed. The impression I had was that he was rubbing his nose into the gravel, grinding away at the hook.

During this stage of the fight the fish never did anything more exciting than to cruise forty or fifty yards round the big back-water, always returning to the same spot. My reel had fifty to ninety yards of line off it all the time, and only once did I succeed in getting the fish near to me. On that occasion I had him in the shallow water twenty yards away and a clever gaffer, willing to take a risk, might have got him. I tried myself, but he sheered off and went back to the old spot. Every trick was used to make him fight harder; rings were put down the line; pebbles, stones, and eventually rocks were thrown at him, but he would not move, and it was quite obvious that he was hooked in a part of the mouth that did not really worry him, for the pressure I had on all the time was constant and as heavy as the gut could stand.

By this time the banks were sprinkled liberally with spectators —some dozen or more of them—and so insistent was the fish in keeping to the other bank, that I had hopes of him getting too near and being gaffed by one of the fishermen on that side. The only way to get a pull from down below seemed to be by using a boat, for the water was too deep for wading except at the tree-fringed edges where it was about neck high. A boat was sent for, but a message came back saying it had gone duck-shooting, so I decided to go in up to my neck and edge down past the trees. This manoeuvre was nearly completed when the fish woke up with a vengence and started fighting hard. At this critical moment my reel chose to jam—a loop of line having got crossed over—and it nearly came to a break, but I got the line free just in time.

The fish was now rolling heavily—after four hours' fighting—and I could see his deep silvery-purple side and once, when his head came out for a brief moment, I caught a glimpse of that appallingly fine gut coming from his mouth.

I decided he would have to come over to my side before we got to the pull of the main Mount Pool, for I could not risk a half-baked monster being carried down by the current—out of control, and much beyond the strength of my gut to hold—so, just above the stile, I gave him all the pressure I dared. I worked him to within six feet of the two gaffers who were waiting and they, fearing to make a false stroke at such a fish, missed their one and only chance; they stayed motionless, waiting for him to come that extra foot, but he did not like the look of them, and the extra strain of the short line was a shade too much for the overstrained gut; it parted at 2.30—four hours and ten minutes after the hooking, and I threw my rod to the ground without so much as a 'Damn'. It was a moment I do not ever want repeated. The fish was practically finished—and so was I. What was his weight? Who knows? The gaffers went off muttering, 'well over forty', and I have my own idea too, but we shall never know. I have had fish up to 35 lb since that day, and I can only say that he was *very much* larger.

Note. This incident happened in the very early days of mono-filament development when the material on sale was subject to most extraordinary faults. I lost many salmon, and a number of large trout at Blagdon, due to a peculiar weakness which resulted in a fracture some three inches from the fly when the line was not under any great stress. My friend Dr Stanley Barnes, who subsequently wrote a book on nylon monofilament, carried out a great number of tests, and had much discussion with the makers on the subject. The material was eventually improved and this structural fault eliminated, but it made the angler very dubious about using it for some time, so some of us returned to using gut.

Chapter 5

The Villains
and some of Their Tricks

I NEVER MET a fair-minded fishery owner or lessee who, in his heart of hearts, did not rather enjoy hearing of the exploits of the local poacher; even if it cost him a trout or two—subject to the poaching being done by reasonably sporting methods, such as a few casts with the fly, or a bit of worm-dangling. 'Good luck to him! I should not have had the pluck to do it myself,' is the usual reaction.

So let me commence this chapter on the lighter side of poaching and to recount one or two of the more amusing happenings I have come across.

I have done but little sea-trout fishing, and that by day. I have the greatest respect for the sporting qualities of this game fish, but do not really enjoy fishing at nights, the best time for this branch of angling. Apart from the usual nocturnal hazards of barbed wire, sleeping cows, fallen trees and other obstacles, I miss the beauty of scene, the colours, and the wild life. On the day of which I write I was fishing for sea-trout in west Wales, with only a brace of fish to show for a morning's sport. While enjoying lunch and a rest, I spotted a rather furtive character working along the opposite bank, peering into the river, but not carrying a rod or other visible means of extracting fish. He passed out of sight and left me puzzled.

Some time later I saw the same fellow on my bank, near to a run I was just thinking of fishing. He approached quite unabashed and without any preliminaries offered to sell me a salmon. The conversation went something like this:

'Do you want to buy a fish? I have one of about ten pounds,' said he.

'No, I don't. I've come here to catch sea-trout.'

'That doesn't stop you from buying a nice fresh salmon, does it? You can always say you caught it,' he persisted.

'How did you catch it?' I asked. 'You haven't a rod or a gaff, and I can't see any fish spears about you.'

He laughed. 'I got it the usual way, with a rabbit wire. They're not only useful for catching rabbits, you know.'

He was clearly a likeable rogue, and was quite willing to expound on his technique. 'I'm called Roberts the Fish,' he said, 'and I do a nice business supplying the hotel—and some anglers— with salmon and trout. It pays very well, you know. The fish here have a liking for lying with their noses tucked into the bank. It's simple, if you are quiet, to slip wire over their tails and lift them out—like you gentlemen do with those tailers you carry, but don't often use because I've usually been along before you. Simple, isn't it? Nothing to carry that you can't get rid of quickly if the bailiff comes round.'

I felt depressed. My short holiday looked like producing a blank. The barman had told me that the beat they had on the river had some good runs of fish, and the hotel paid £400 a year for it. How did they expect to keep their angling visitors satisfied if they condoned this state of affairs?

I was not interested in becoming one of the poacher's custo- mers or receivers, so I gave him a couple of shillings for a drink, really to get rid of him. But I fired one last question before he went.

'All this doesn't make sense,' I said. 'How can the hotel please its anglers if it is encouraging you to poach all the fish? Why do they buy from you at all? If they didn't, it would soon put you out of business.'

He was vastly amused at this. When he finished laughing he explained more fully, in the tolerant manner in which you would explain a problem to a child.

'It's like this,' he said, grinning broadly. 'First of all they never catch me, for I work before they are out of bed. Even if they did catch me there is no evidence, for I can drop a rabbit wire and disown it. There are plenty of rabbit catchers round here who

58

could have dropped one. They will never catch me with a fish on me because I have secret places—you know!' (This with a significant grin.) 'Also, I supply all the important people in the town; they like a bit of cheap salmon, and I wouldn't say that some of them are not on the bench—but of course they wouldn't know what their wives buy at the back door,' he added with a sly wink. 'But the most important thing is that the hotel has to feed its customers, and they expect to eat local salmon. The anglers can't supply them, because the few they may catch they want to take home with them. So you see I am really doing everybody a good turn.'

That evening I bought the barman a few drinks and he confirmed all I had been told. What I had *not* been told was that two large deep freeze cabinets in the home of the poacher's father, known locally as 'Roberts the Freezer', stored all the surplus —and that these supplied weddings and other functions in a town some eighteen miles away!

I suppose this happens the world over, but it is a discouraging thought for the holiday angler. The total rod catch at this particular hotel was no more than eighteen for the previous season. I wonder what the count was for the Roberts partnership?

My next experience was again in Wales. I was new to the water and finding my way about it. One of the pools was famous. It was deep and its natural rock sides were steep. The fishing was from a pathway along the top. It was a great taking and resting pool.

While fishing it down I was astonished to see a nice fish turn up a few yards in front of me. It rolled over slowly several times and showed line marks round its body quite clearly. I was a bit too proper, and a lot too slow. I did not quite know how the lady owner would view it, if I was seen gaffing an unattached fish with an ornate design of line-markings round his body. I need not have worried. While I was pondering the matter, my gaff was torn off my back and before you could blink an eyelid a seventeen-pounder was on the bank. The local who had materialised from nowhere said, 'There you are. Your day. Your fish.' He was quite unabashed about it all. 'I fished here last night. Had two and lost this one'! He did not explain the winding-marks, and I did not ask. It was all too obvious.

The following week-end I was asked to go up to the big house to see a large fish caught that afternoon. 'Thirty-five pounds— and I caught it on a tiny one-inch minnow,' said the owner. I looked it over but did not see any suspicious marks on the body. Perhaps they were on the other side, but you can't be rude, can you, and roll it over as though you were looking for something! A few days later a friend fishing a sink-and-draw prawn in the same pool got hung up on the bottom. He was using a powerful line, but even with that it seemed that a break was inevitable. However, he persisted and eventually recovered a device unlike any he had seen before; a treble with hooks on it $1\frac{1}{2}$ in. in the gape, and with a large lump of lead at the junction. It was attached to picture cord, and he came to the obvious conclusion. This used to be a fairly common way of fishing deep gorges and it does not seem to have died out.

I suppose there will always be scope for the 'dirty tricks department' in all forms of sport (and in politics, too!) and there are degrees of villainy. The batsman who moves his feet a couple of inches after being given out lbw; stares incredulously at the umpire's raised finger; looks down at his legs, then at the wicket, and slowly and reluctantly retires with his head wagging in disbelief is practising 'gamesmanship'. But the footballer who charges into a dangerous and illegal tackle, knowing that a serious injury may result, is guilty of a much more serious offence which is deserving of punishment.

So it is with poachers. The solitary countryman who poaches a fish for his supper can be viewed with some degree of tolerance. He is very often 'a bit of a character', an amusing raconteur—and very good company with a pint in his hand! Frequently his brushes with authority are as much enjoyed by the magistrate as they are by the offender.

Personally, the poachers I could do really unpleasant things to are the scoundrels that steal fish from the couple of miles of local trout stream on which I have one of three tickets. It is a delightful fly water, small and difficult to wade and fish. It is first-class in the Mayfly and deserves better treatment than it often gets.

Set lines are the usual method of poaching. A length of nylon tied to an underwater root and baited with a worm. The wading angler only finds them when a dead trout is seen lying on the bottom. When it is picked up it is found to be attached to the line.

The difficulty is to catch the poachers with the trout on them. They are very clever at getting rid of the evidence. The water bailiff usually has plenty of other work to keep him busy and is really only interested in the man who fishes without a River Authority Licence. Like me, he is getting on a bit and is incapable of catching young poachers tearing uphill like greyhounds. It just cannot be done. Consequently, it is no unusual thing for me to know that trout are for sale in a certain pub. My trout. I know the number of fish, the names of the sellers, the name of the receiver, and the price paid, and yet such is the law that the police cannot do anything about it. It appears that offenders must be caught in the act and with the stolen property in their possession.

When I say they are quick in getting rid of the evidence I mean it. Very quick. I had a salmon pool at the end of the garden of my previous house and poachers could creep along under a wall so that I could not see them from my windows. One day I thought I saw the tip of a rod flash and dashed down with a long gaff I had grabbed hastily. As I looked over the edge I saw this villain. I gradually pushed out the gaff until it was only inches from his pants. In another couple of seconds he was going to get an unpleasant pain in his backside, but the telepathy or whatever it is that warns men of danger flashed in his brain, he whipped round and saw me. What did he do? Did he run away? Not on your life. He bent down to a rock where he had two good trout concealed and threw them into the river—and then he ran. I went after him, but he dashed across the river. What could I have done had I caught him? Nothing.

On another occasion, I saw three scruffy-looking characters fishing in the same place. I phoned the police and we caught them. What was the result? Two got away without even a warning because they had licences and no fish, and the other 'angler' was fined 30/- for not having a licence. It transpired his wages were £40 a week!

As far as I can see you must take the remedy in your own hands in dealing with poachers. I found a man fishing one day, and as I approached from perhaps a hundred yards away he concealed his rod amongst the boulders and walked off smartly. I hunted around and had great difficulty in finding the rod, but in the end I did. I took off the reel and threw it into the deep part of the pool and walked along the rod half-a-dozen times. That was all I could do, and that was in all probability illegal.

I hope that what I have written so far under this chapter-heading will give the impression that we anglers are, in general, a fairly even-tempered community. We tolerate, even with some amusement, the solitary poacher seeking his supper; we have (understandably!) rather more dislike for the human predators who poach from our own fishing waters; we condemn wholeheartedly the mass-poachers whose only motive is that of amassing a huge profit—a crime against conservationists and anglers alike—but we reserve a real hatred for those evil men who use explosives to bomb the pools, and who put poison into the tributaries. For such men there can be no adequate punishment.

Do I have a pet hate? Yes, I do—and I find it difficult to write in a detached way about those who, in my opinion, are the worst possible offenders. Here I am referring to the anglers who should know better—in many instances educated and professional men—but men nevertheless responsible for grave transgressions which get honest anglers into disrepute. One hears and reads of their unsportsmanlike conduct but still finds it difficult to understand what possible pleasure they can get out of pursuing their devious methods of fishing.

On the Tweed, for instance, during the late season fly-only period, there is usually a good run of fish which may be seen without difficulty in the clear water. It might occur to a ten-year-old, or to a starving man searching for a meal, that these fish could be foul hooked and dragged ashore, but one shudders at the realisation that well-educated men posing as anglers can sink so low for their 'sport'—and yet they do, on this and other rivers. The sport of Snatching!

Heavy leaded lines are permitted at Grafham and some other

fisheries for getting a line down to the bottom of the deepest parts of the lake for the purpose of presenting large lures, resembling small fish, to the largest trout which have become bottom feeders. Many fish are caught by this method and they are usually fairly hooked in the mouth. It is obvious that the despicable pot hunter can use such techniques, with a heavy and sparsely dressed tube fly fitted with a substantial treble, to snatch beautiful salmon—most of them fresh fish which have run the gauntlet of predators, nets, and all the other perils of salt water.

It is all very disgusting, and unfair to the true angler. An article in *Trout and Salmon* of June 1975 makes it clear that this practice has very nearly resulted in the prohibition of permits. That such a possibility exists, simply because of the activities of these men, is enough to enrage the most benign of anglers!

So how do we deal with the villains in our midst? There is no easy solution. Since the value of the pound fell and wages soared, the sentences imposed on all forms of poachers are derisory. It is certainly no deterrent for the bench to impose a fine of a pound or two; much heavier penalties are essential.

Is it too much to hope that we may eventually get laws as sensible as the Scots, which permit confiscation of everything appertaining to the poaching—whether it be cars, guns, rods or any other item of equipment contributing to the offence? A speedy revision of our out-dated legislation is clearly needed.

Chapter 6

River and Brook Trout

IT IS ALL a matter of opinion—and opportunity, I suppose! If you are the owner of a length of chalk stream, or have sufficient wealth to rent one, you are indeed blessed, for the charms and delights of chalk stream fishing, and the many difficulties to be overcome, are unique. It is regrettable that the pressures of modern fishing have made the stocking of rainbows necessary—splendid, hard-fighting fish that they are—simply in order to keep pace with the hammering most of these rivers get. The native brown trout, many of which were admittedly artificially raised in close proximity to the water into which they were to be released, seemed to fit into the scene more naturally, and no doubt many of the splendid old anglers and writers of seventy or more years ago would be absolutely shattered to see the way things have gone. One blessing is that both rainbows and brownies very soon become acclimatised and it does not take them long to be selective both in the lies they take over, and the menu which suits their taste. The bad side of the coin is the habit of so many pressurised tycoons of setting about these poor fish within twenty-four hours of their release, and amassing large bags with the nearest fly they can make or buy having a strong resemblance to a small piece of liver, horsemeat, or a pellet. I suppose it sounds so impressive, over one's gin and tonic in the club, to announce casually, 'I had four brace of nice rainbows, 22 lb, on an odd-looking nymph'.

Of course, sour grapes can very easily enter into these observations, and that would be regrettable, but if you have been fortunate enough to have had a little of each kind of trout fishing as I have: chalk streams, border streams, rain fed and full of problems such as high banks and timber, and lakes of various sizes, from some excellent small,˙clear lakes of two or three acres, to the big expanses such as Blagdon, Chew, and many of the other well-known ticket waters, you have been blessed with a taste of them all, and should be able to express an un-biased opinion on English trout waters. I emphasise English, because the Irish loughs have characters and difficulties all of their own, and shall be the subject of a few remarks later on.

It may be that I prefer the fishing for the small trout of the Welsh border stream because I have lived near to this region and have fished these charming brooks and rivers for over fifty years. I don't think I have ever caught a two-pounder from any of them and if you want large fish you must seek elsewhere. The chalk streams and the lakes are full of them. Half-pounders are the general size of fish in our baskets, with fewer three-quarter-pounders and just one or two real monsters of from 14 oz to a pound-and-a-half if you are very lucky, and if you fish the slower and almost impossible places. These fish are all wild and are very active fighters, resisting until the last moment, and what is more, they can be guaranteed to be good eaters. A Ledwyche, Upper Lugg, or Teme trout, cooked under the grill with a rasher of ham, or lightly smoked, is something you could not match in the best hotels.

In one of my last books, written in the latter years of the Second World War, I refer to the fishing in the chalk streams. Since then my fishing has all been in the border streams and the lakes, so I shall confine my present remarks to them. Things have changed in some repects, mostly in tackle and only very little in methods or flies, but in fact there is little to add to what I then wrote. Essentially, the hollow fibre-glass rod, the plastic line, and the monofilament leader are the important changes, and what a blessing they have been.

The rivers and brooks within thirty miles of the Welsh border can mostly be fished enjoyably with a 7 ft fibre-glass rod, a No. 5 floater for dry fly, or sinker tip for wet, and a 6 ft leader with a point added, 1½ to 3 lb. An excellent heavily-tapered leader is Tom Saville's No Gleam knotless taper fly cast. Butt 0·017 in.

tapering to 4X. I always made up my own leaders with heavy tapers for dry-fly, but this involved many blood-knots and there is no doubt that numerous knots cause casting snarls, which are far less frequent when knotless tapers are used. A point of some 16 in. is tied on and replaced when necessary, leaving the Saville cast its original length. For wet fly or two nymphs, a 20 in. point, with a dropper tied in, is satisfactory.

Because many of the brooks are small and heavily treed and bushed it should not be assumed that they are miniature rivers needing only lighter tackle and shorter rods. Far from it. They are much more exhausting, and as they very often run between high and precipitous banks they require the dexterity of an active young man—preferably sired by a mountain goat! They are certainly a grave problem for (what are we called nowadays?) senior citizens with rheumatism and slipped discs. The easiest way to cope with the problem is to stay in the river and walk its length as far as possible. Trouser waders are necessary for this, but they are also really essential for other reasons. Eighty per cent of the craft of fishing such waters is to remain still and to make oneself as harmonious with the surroundings as can be achieved.

The little fellows are the bane of the border angler's life. These tiddlers tear upstream when you wade to your position, no matter how cautious you may be, sending all their seniors to cover, and as you would expect, the biggies take longer to recover from such shocks, so you may as well forget that pool and move on to the next, giving them some time to settle. These tiddlers are a great problem to which I have no solution—though I did mention the element of luck earlier in the book!

You may, with very good reason, be at a loss to know where and how to start on your arrival at a trout stream. Do you put up a dry fly and fish on the top; or a wet fly or some nymph-like creature to fish just under the surface, or some kind of lightly leaded nymph to get down to the bottom? It is a bewildering problem when first you start fishing. But if you think it over, standing on a bridge or a bank and using your eyes, it is not all that confusing.

If trout are rising here and there and are obviously sipping, sucking or seizing flies from the surface it is pretty obvious.

What is not quite so obvious is the rise which looks as if it breaks the surface to seize a fly, but does not actually do so. It makes a nice swirl, looking like a surface rise, but a really keen eye will see that some mysterious unseen thing is being sucked in just below the surface, and the actual surface or skin of the water remains unbroken. In that case use a little wet fly, say a small Williams' Favourite, or one of Mrs Sawyer's little nymphs fished to sink just a few inches. You do this by spitting on the fly to soak it, leaving 6 in. of nylon nearest the fly to sink, and rubbing the remainder of the leader with a buoyant grease such as Mucilin. That will present it at about the level required.

If nothing at all is seen rising or 'bulging' you can only assume that fish are grubbing about on the bottom, which they very often are, or are right off the feed for the time being. This may be due to unsettled weather or water conditions, or other upsets like otters, mink, poachers, or a hundred other things.

In this event, try fishing a leaded fly or nymph right down deep by using a leader rubbed with clay or mud, or Fuller's Earth, or some de-greaser out of the kitchen, and work the lure about the bottom very slowly.

Try them all. Be patient. You might sit down for an hour and not see a thing. When all hope is gone, some of us have a strong belief in the efficacy of starting to pour a drink from the Thermos. Fish love to rise at the precise moment when confusion will be most marked. It *always* worked in our old pike-fishing days. Out came the Thermos and down went the float!

Long casts are not called for in this type of fishing, but variety is helpful. Much of it is switching and dibbling, and the underhand switch is perhaps the most useful cast of all. There is no need for casting elaborate 'shepherds' crooks' and suchlike things to catch these trout, but there is need to throw plenty of slack. Drag is ever-present and every little run has its problems. Fish love lying in tails, and those fish are most difficult to catch. If you throw up from the fast run below the tail you have immediate drag, and if you throw from the side with a cross-country, or rather, cross-pebble cast, it is only for a moment or two that the fly is presented properly and an almost immediate lift is necessary. The fish only has a split second to get hooked, but the gamble sometimes comes off.

It is probably better to concentrate on the slacker parts of the stream near the banks and under the alders. A well-floating fly is needed and it should be left on the surface until it comes downstream to only a few yards above you. It is surprising how many fish follow down and take at the last moment. It is also surprising the language these alders call forth!

In this type of fishing you are almost bound to have difficulties. It is no use losing your temper. I have friends whose bull-like bellow could be heard fifty yards away. Alders are the very devil and so are tufts of tough, dried, last-season's grasses on the banks. If your fly lands in such places go about recovery in a very quiet manner. A slow draw often results in a miraculous release, but if you have seen the fly do a trapeze act round an alder-berry it is all up. The wood might break, but it is odds that you will lose your fly—and it is always a special fly you have tied with great care!

On many such streams (I have the upper Lugg in mind as I write) there is a hole, and very often a deep one, wherever the stream turns a corner. Such places can trap an unwary wader, particularly should he be a short man, because the bottom is often of sloping loose gravel which displaces as you sink. These spots always hold good trout and the fish usually venture out into adjacent feeding stations, particularly in the evening. Needless to say, an Alder type of fly, anything black with a ribbed peacock herl body is acceptable, and many a monster of a pound has come from such places.

Never, never, use one of those collapsing triangular folding telescopic landing nets. A net of any kind is an infernal nuisance in this type of fishing, but the folding sorts are invariably jammed by reason of all the grasping briars and other fishermen's burdens which entangle with them, and the clip comes off on the bank or in the river. A plain old-fashioned ring on a wading stick or cane is the thing. No trouble at all, and if you arrange it on a sling over your shoulders with a running ring to carry it you can use it as a wading staff, which in this type of water is an absolute necessity. It is more necessary on the Teme, where rock ledges can drop you from two feet into twenty in one step. Sling an ordinary fishmonger's frail, about 18 in. by 13 in. round your neck to carry the fish and keep them fresh. No plastic bags on any account, and you will have all you need for brook fishing. The same equipment does for the larger rivers but an 8 ft or 8 ft 6 in. rod might help just in case you get taken by a very large chub or the occasional salmon. In anticipation of the latter happy turn of events it is a good idea to carry a small gaff in the frail. (Not one of those toy things, but one about 2½ in. in the gape lashed on to a short handle.)

There is one very good thing to be said about these twisty little brooks. On most days, wherever the wind might blow from, you can find calm and shelter, with more than a possibility of a few rising fish.

When you have overcome the difficulties of wading, casting and landing fish from a brook you are not very far from knowing how to tackle larger rivers. It is all much the same, but the larger rivers are usually much more open and are far easier. The streams, giides, runs and backwaters are all somewhat magnified and the slightly longer rod helps to overcome drag and such-like problems. It may be worth mentioning an obvious fact here, but it is one that is often overlooked. The low rod, pointing almost at the fly, which we use on the chalk streams and lakes, is not suitable on confused rivers where the streams come in and depart from the main run at all kinds of angles. A rod held low leaves too much line on the water surface and this results in more and faster drag. A rod held higher, but not too high to strike a fish, lifts much of the line from the surface with consequently less drag. I suggest an angle of about 60° from the water surface. It makes quite a difference.

These little wild brownies are often quick on the take. They are away into the banks and tree roots as soon as they feel the hook. Don't treat them too gently. Firm handling will save you many a loss.

And now we come to that vexed question: flies!

This is where a writer can drop into all kinds of trouble. For some reason it seems to be a very sensitive matter with certain anglers. To omit their pet fly, or to extol one which they condemn, is regarded as a personal insult.

The columns of the fishing journals burn with the fury of their views. They verge on heart attacks over such world-shattering questions as the exact shade of yellow tag in a Treacle Parkin, or whether or not a fluorescent tag is better than a bit of wool out of grandpa's old bed-sock, in a Red Tag. I will stir something up by voicing a personal opinion. I have tied dozens of flies with fluorescent materials to try out this wonder material. I can honestly say that I have never had even a pluck on any of them. It cannot be just my lack of skill in that particular direction, because a change to the orthodox pattern has immediately produced results. Perhaps this stuff is only for brightening up the lives of fishes living in deep, dark gloomy lakes. If so, I apologise to the trout of my stream for dazzling them. And, I might add to the fluorescent addicts before they charge me with the obvious, 'You used too much of it', that I only used the tiniest morsels. Also, I tried the flies on widely differing days; dull, bright, cold, hot—all of them.

I have been disillusioned on numerous occasions, as I expect we all have if we are honest, by the fact that the fish have not read their Halford. Many of my flies have looked to me even better than the natural. Yet the fish would have none of them. Then, having tried all reasonable and appetising recipes I have gone mad and tied on a horror twice the obvious size; sombre, uninteresting, and lacking sex or any other appeal. But the fish thought otherwise. It was just what they had been waiting for. Why? I have a nasty feeling that we, the exact imitators, are sometimes right, depending on light and many scientific things, but we are more often very wrong and that it is the pattern created by the legs of the floating fly on the surface, and its outline, which matter most. Perhaps the glint of ribbing means something too.

If there is some logic in this argument it would seem to follow that the need for exact imitation is far greater in the wet fly than in the dry. I personally incline to this view and regard the old snobbery of the supremacy of the dry fly as very doubtful. I would almost go so far as to say that dry fly fishing is the simplest form of angling, apart from the floodwater worm and such-like lowly horribles, and the wet fly requires much more knowledge— skill in fly-dressing, exactitude of presentation, and water craft.

The surface of the water would seem to be the dividing line between impressionism and exact imitation, only it is the wrong way up. The old snobbery held that the dry fly must be exact, and the wet fly could be any old thing. The truth could be the reverse. Anyhow, my trout, up to a point, agree with me. Granted, they will not accept a whacking great Alder when they are sipping in tiny gnats and such-like little animals; that is to be expected. But they don't worry much whether a well-tied fly with fine shiny hackles is a Pheasant Tail, Dogsbody, or Blue Dun. If they need a snack they take it and if they don't, or if they have just had a nasty experience with another angler, they just ignore it.

I think therefore that half-a-dozen of each of the following well-tied dry flies should find a home in the brook angler's pocket. Sizes from 10 to 14.

First of all, a fly I tied experimentally forty years ago and have usually done well with on border streams. Hook 12/14. A good strong black tail to stop the rear end sinking and the fly fishing tail down. Body: peacock bronze herb, Ribbing: red floss twisted tight, and a couple of really good shiny black cock's hackles. I have killed trout on this fly in all kinds of waters: Test, Itchen, Welsh streams, Midland rivers, lakes and pools. They take it all through the spring and summer seasons. Call it what you like.

Dogsbody; Gold-ribbed Hare's Ear; Dark Olive; Hawthorn (a big fly, black all over, with long rather untidy hackles, not over-stiff, very good in April and May); Blue Dun; Coch-y-bonddu; Pheasant Tail; Grey Duster; Greenwell's Glory; Red Quill; Flight's Fancy; Red Tag; Sedges of various sizes, and Houghton Ruby.

The Mayfly has as many forms and admirers as the ladies of the old *Folies Bergère*. Each angler and every river and stream has its favourites. Three years ago I went out to commence the Mayfly season armed with all and sundry, collected over many years. Some of them killed fish and some did not. Those which killed fish one day gave up their lead to the non-killers on the following day, and so on. There seemed to be no reason to it. Amongst the flies were half-a-dozen which I had just tied. They were very simple and very effective. Veniards, or Tom Saville Ltd., who incidently give splendid service, will send you hollow plastic Mayfly bodies and these I have found to be very acceptable to the fish. They look like a Mayfly body, and very often you will see a fish following them down and giving a critical examination. They usually make their last mistake! Order those bodies which are not pierced at the rear end to take a tail. There is no need for this tail. It is laid down that pheasant tail fibres should be put in and cemented, but this is far from being essential. They take them very well without any tail. Tie them with waxed silk to a wide gape No. 12 hook. See that they are full of air, and then put varnish or Durafix on the binding and make sure the whole thing is airtight. Then put a couple of good badger hackles on to cover the binding and finish off with the usual four-turn whip. I have found them to be good killers, and with the small hooks used they float well. If you tie them on to large or heavy hooks it is rather a gamble as to whether the air-filled body, or the hook, wins the buoyancy battle. Last year I did not carry any other pattern and the fish took them well.

It is worth mentioning that, on these border streams at any rate, you should not regard the Mayfly as only a fly for the limited period of the Mayfly hatch, as it is generally accepted in the south. There can be driblets of fly coming down for a long time after the usual period, and after a good rest following the main hatch, the fish may come on the take again. In fact I have found that they frequently take better in these later hatches. After our late May and early June hatches last year the fly seemed to be finished, but to my surprise they resumed hatching in the latter half of July and, what is more, the fish took them really well. On the two rather hurried visits I paid to the stream I threw Mayflies to fifteen fish and every one took.

The small list of flies I have suggested will catch fish on border streams and brooks. I have no doubt that many other selections chosen by anglers with differing ideas would do just as well. This type of fishing calls for a fly which will float well, sitting up on the tips of its hackles if it is for fishing the streams and quiet backwaters under the bushes. Such flies as the Hare's Ear fish in the surface film and the Hawthorn sometimes does good work when it is fished awash. I feel sure that presentation, fine nylon points, and patience in allowing the fly to fish the full length of the holding water, are more important matters than exact imitation. And, once again, the angler should emulate the heron—stand very still!

Wet fly fishing is, in my opinion, a more difficult art to master than dry fly. Many people think that to cast a fly roughly in the downstream direction, and to hold on leaving the fly to fish itself on the dangle is wet fly fishing. Far from it. As in skilled spinning, depth is an important matter, and a full knowledge of the formation of the river bed is essential. On rocky and ledgy rivers and streams it is most difficult to present a fly so that it passes a given lie—say a stone—at the right speed, in the right stream to carry it along, and at the correct depth. This must be far more difficult than presenting the dry fly. The dry fly angler will be inclined to reply to this statement by saying, 'Ah, but what about drag?' Unnatural drag is just as off-putting to a trout below the water surface, as on the top. Granted the under-water flies are tumbled downstream in a rough and turbulent manner, but they follow the natural run of the water, and if your artificial does not do this, it is suspect.

It is therefore necessary to cast up, across, or sometimes almost downstream in an effort to achieve this natural presentation, and that is no easy matter. The really good wet fly fisher learns from experience how to fish his flies bearing all these difficulties in mind.

The flies for this kind of fishing must very obviously look like hatching nymphs, drowned flies, or the creatures that normally go about the business of life underwater. My experience is that the flies tied and used north of the midlands, very precisely and lightly dressed, are the ones to use. It is difficult (at least I have found it so) to tie them as sparsely as the northerners do. The midlands and Welsh border tradition has been towards a more meaty and bulky fly, and in the case of dry flies this pays dividends, for the rain-fed border brooks do not have the tremendous fly hatches of the chalk streams and a good mouthful appeals to trout that have to scratch for a living—at any rate during the spring months.

The delicate bodies and sparse hackles of the northerners are combined with an accuracy of colour and tone which produces a fly that looks extraordinarily like a natural morsel being swept downstream. They are mostly tied on very small hooks. Nos. 14, 16 and 18 are, in certain conditions, excellent. When the water carries a bit of colour, however, it is wise to have a few No. 12s in your box.

Many times on these streams I tried the flies which have brought success on lakes, streams and rivers, but never with good results. Those little Freeman's Fancies, Small Claret and Mallards, Dunkelds, Invictas, do not appeal. They are too stiff and unnatural, and yet they catch fish in lakes where there is even less current to activate the feathers!

There are anglers, however, who swear by such flies. I was recommended to use a small Butcher for grayling on the Upper Teme. Yet I only caught one fish on it. Changing to a very lightly dressed Treacle Parkin I got fish almost at once. Each angler seems to have a small selection of flies which are his favourites and with which he does best. In a few words, this amounts to faith and confidence.

Useful wet flies for fishing a wide range of rivers and streams include the following; some of them lightly tied in the north country tradition. Williams' Favourite, Greenwell's Glory, Steel Blue, Rough Olive, Waterhen Quill, Treacle Parkin, Snipe and Orange, Snipe and Purple, Silver Twist, Red Tag. These are useful for clear water conditions and should be fished on nylon not exceeding 2½ lb b.s. Tied larger and fuller they are useful spring flies on any of the Shropshire, Hereford or Welsh border streams.

When we come to nymphs and nymph fishing, we are entering a most delightful and fascinating branch of the sport. Although the nymph is fished below the surface it is perhaps more akin to dry-fly fishing, than wet. Major Oliver Kite who, sadly, died at an early age, left us, amongst others, a most delightful and informative little book which covers every aspect of this particular branch of the sport. He was an authority on the subject and I recommend that his invaluable little book, published in 1965 by Herbert Jenkins, *Elements of Nymph Fishing*, should be in every angler's library—or better still, in every angler's pocket until he has absorbed every word of it. It is an intriguing book which will help an angler catch many of those difficult trout in the summer months and will also impart the secrets of catching grayling in the autumn months. This is far from being an easy method of fishing. It requires much patience, careful study and also the physical attributes of a very keen eye, and a quick response by the hand holding the rod. The nymph fisherman should also read all the works of G. E. M. Skues.

Should you wish to try your hand with the nymph prior to learning how to construct one which is likely to fool the trout, I recommend you to send for a range of Mrs Sawyer's splendid home-made patterns. I have done well with them. You will find her advertisements in *Trout and Salmon*.

Before concluding this brief chapter on trout fishing in our delightful streams I should like to list a few items which will, I think, add to your pleasure and comfort.

Boxes: to keep your flies neat and in good condition are essential: spring-top boxes, or boxes with magnetic strips to hold dry flies, and flat-50 size cigarette tins, with felt pads stuck in to them for wet flies and nymphs. A plain empty box should also be in your bag or pocket to hold used flies so that they don't damp the unused ones.

Pins: especially those round-headed ones they put in new shirts, should find a place in your lapels to clear the eyes in flies. If you forget this tip, use the hook of another fly—but a pin is easier.

Scissors: of which the blunt-ended pairs of Hardy's are the best. Quite essential.

Wasp-eze: magnificent stuff in a small aerosol. It removes all fear of wasp stings, horsefly bites, nettle stings, jelly-fish stings—in fact all the horrors of the out of doors in summer. From Boots or other chemists.

Priests: a small priest is essential to crack your fish on the head. I hate that business of pushing your thumb down their throats and bending their heads back, and what is more, they remain disfigured.

Cloth: don't forget a good rough-textured cloth on which you can wipe your hands.

Fly dope: those damned flies—especially the horseflies. What a curse they are! I have run through most of the modern sprays, lotions and ointments to repel them, and there is not a chemist's shop within miles I have not visited. Some of the new things seem to work, then somehow they fail. I am now back on my old Citronella and Paraffin. It is not too unpleasant a smell, and it does the trick in the moderate climate of England. I would not like to guarantee it in the real midge plague spots, like Finland and even parts of Scotland.

In at least one respect I am peculiar. (My friends will think of many more!) Having for many years searched the rivers for the largest trout, I have now decided that whilst looking for the big fellows from a sporting point of view I tend to prefer the ½ and ¾ pounders to eat, and in consequence many of the larger fish go back to improve the average size for the water. In the smaller streams and brooks the half-pounder is the more normal size and likely to be in the peak of condition. Although the pounders are almost as good I find there is a slight falling off in flavour. It really depends on the food supply to some extent, and also the fact that many of the larger fish tend to lie in the backwaters and quiet spots under willows, which are lacking the sparkle of the haunts of smaller trout.

These remarks are not intended to apply to clear water lakes or chalk streams where the food supply and the quality of the water maintain an average size of, say, 2 lb or perhaps more. Those fish usually eat remarkably well at about those sizes, but there are exceptions, and these are horrible!

A note or two on the cooking of trout may not be out of place. There are few better breakfasts than a couple of half-pound trout, a rasher of ham, and two or three mushrooms.

The trout, caught the day before, should be washed, then dried and opened, the entire contents being removed. Use the thumb nail, or one of the now rare potbrushes (the best instrument) for getting all traces of colour away from the vertebrae. Do not wash the inside; dry it with a cloth, then salt and leave it all night. Grill in whatever fat you prefer, dripping from beef being best. Turn frequently, and cook well. Trout which are undercooked do not leave the bone well and can be too firm.

There are many other ways and one of the best is smoking in an ABU smoker. This process is extremely simple and trout can be smoked and ready to serve hot on the table in ten minutes. Full instructions are supplied and the only additional suggestion I can make is that the sawdust is kept to a minimum—just a sprinkle is enough. Smoked trout can be served cold and are very tasty.

Another excellent recipe is 'Trout à la Meuniere'. This is a form of frying, and the fish is prepared exactly as advised for grilled trout. Cleaned, dried and lightly salted, if possible the day previously. If this is not possible it is quite satisfactory to eat the same day as caught, although I always think the flavour is improved by allowing the salt some hours to penetrate. Flour the trout. Heat some butter until it starts simmering in the frying pan. Put the trout therein and cook on gentle heat, turning as necessary.

Prior to dishing up, sprinkle a good pinch of finely-chopped parsley into the frying pan. When dishing up, pour the butter/parsley mixture, which will have browned slightly, over the fish and add a bit of extra chopped parsley. A touch of lemon should be served with it, to add a piquant flavour.

A dish of half- to three-quarter-pound trout, or grayling, cooked in this manner, accompanied by a good Riesling, is indeed a dish worth while. Grayling should be treated in exactly the same manner as trout, but should be scraped and scaled first. In some opinions they are just as good as trout.

In this debatable matter of taste it is rather difficult to be specific, for tastes vary so much. A very beautiful lake of some five or six acres, a delightful spot, with a great variety of birds and trees, produces the most evil-tasting trout it has been my misfortune to meet at table. This is an old lake and it originally held coarse fish. A friend who fished there forty years ago tells me that even in those days the pike and eels were impossible to eat. This lake was emptied some years ago and was found to be thick with mud of an evil-smelling nature, no doubt caused by rotting leaves from the trees surrounding it. It was left fallow and later on stocked with trout. Beautiful 1 lb to 3 lb fish were introduced and within a week they were impossible to eat. There is a fair but variable inflow, but this crosses a bog, and goodness knows what is spread on the farmland surrounding it. So it is essential to be sure that the trout you cook are from pure fresh water.

Chapter 7

Grayling

A SPLENDID FISH. A fish with so much to commend it that it is something of a mystery why it seems to be loved from the English midlands to the north, where it is appreciated for the sport it gives just when the salmon and trout seasons end, and hated by certain anglers in the south. It is accused of crowding out the trout. Perhaps to some extent it does. Certainly it needs controlling; but that does not justify its classification as 'vermin'.

The south country angler does not have quite so much to contend with in the way of pests as we do. Mink are one of the greatest problems at the present time; and if grayling are pests, likely to consume vast quantities of food, what about the shoals of barbel which have appeared in recent years in the Severn, and are now spreading to the Teme and other similar rivers? They are a problem. I liken them to battalions of vacuum cleaners sucking up everything edible from the river bed, and not rising once to fly to justify their existence! And as for the culinary aspect of the argument, the grayling is a delicate and well-flavoured fish, whereas the barbel is worse than impossible.

Yet, we have to put up with those people (including many who should know better) who are unlawfully and stupidly transferring these pests from one river to another, and increasing their already phenomenal and disastrous spread.

So far as catching the grayling is concerned, if you can catch trout you can catch grayling. The only real difference is that they are less predictable. Some mornings you cannot fail to catch them, other days they are near the surface sucking in everything but your fly. Then there are the frustrating times when all the conditions look good, but never a fish shows.

Nymphing for grayling is good fun and Major Oliver Kite's book tells you all about it. The strange notion, handed down from ages past, that grayling have tender mouths and come unstuck in the playing is so transparently stupid that it makes one realise that some anglers will believe anything. (In the last year I have met pike anglers on local rivers who still chop the dorsal fins off perch live baits.) The grayling's mouth is about as tender as a tractor tyre.

In one respect grayling are easier to catch in numbers than trout. They are shoal fish and once you have located a shoal feeding either on the surface, just under it, or deep down, you might, with caution, take six or eight before they move off or go down.

The grayling of the Teme and other border rivers and streams run to about ½ lb to 1½ lb in weight, but this does not mean that there are not 2½ and 3 pounders deep down, refusing to rise. Their dark shadows can be seen on many a day of clear water and good light penetration. The last time I fished for grayling I was picking up a few from a shoal lying in one of the easy glides they love, using a slow-sinking line to get the flies or nymphs well down to the bottom on the cold and misty November day which gave us our first real chance after a period of heavy rain and high water. Suddenly a heavy fish took and nearly emptied my reel on the first run down and across stream. I thought I had hooked a salmon or foul-hooked a pike and was not too pleased about it. With a 2 lb b.s. leader I knew I had but little hope of landing it. After some five minutes of really heavy runs the fish began to tire, and came up to the surface occasionally. It soon became apparent that it was a very large grayling which I had foul-hooked in the pectoral fin. It is hard to form an accurate estimate, but 2½ to 3 lb was my guess just before the hook came away. A big fish for this part of the country. Undoubtedly these large fish are here, but they do not come to the fly.

Izaak Walton, that wise old fisher, summed up the grayling, and fishing for him, in very few words.

'He grows not to the bigness of a trout; for the biggest of them do not usually exceed eighteen inches, he lives in such rivers as the trout does, and is usually taken with the same bait as the trout is, and after the same manner.'

Grayling take orthodox trout flies and occasionally prefer a modest dowdy little fly, but as a general rule I think it is safe to say that they appreciate a bit of glint and colour. Gay little flies such as a dry Green Insect, or a wet Dunkeld will often stir them into taking, when the drab flies don't give results.

Many anglers complain that grayling nose the dry fly rather than take it. On occasions they certainly do, but I have had splendid days when they have taken the dry fly really firmly. But they are fussy. They will nuzzle and poke at one pattern of fly without meaning business, and yet a very similar fly, but one or two sizes smaller, will be taken firmly and well. Sometimes it is a fraction of gold tag that appears to make them take, or perhaps a nice little green peacock body with just a hint of gold ribbing. You never quite know how they will react to the surface fly; a lick, or a rub between wet fingers to sink the fly may make all the difference. The fly will be taken well and truly as it travels along partly submerged in the surface film. Grayling are very unpredictable but very delightful fish to catch—and don't let anybody tell you they don't fight! A pounder, a dozen yards below you in a Teme ford, with his big dorsal fin practically doubling his purchase on the water, will be a really tough, long-fighting antagonist.

I would suggest that the surest, if the term is permissible when dealing with such a temperamental creature, way to catch grayling is by means of a two- or three-fly cast of wet flies—very slightly leaded, fished across and down, with a slow sinking line. Anyway, that is the combination which suits our particular rivers. Others may require a quick sinker. I am particular, when dressing my flies, not to incorporate too much lead in the bodies, because I think it reduces your sport considerably if you fish a lifeless fly. I much prefer to get down deep by means of the sinking line, leaving the fly to respond to all the little runs and eddies of the stream deep down.

If you carry your boxes of trout dry flies, wet flies and nymphs you will find many patterns which will suit the graylings' appetite.

For wet-fly fishing, whatever your own particular fancy may

be, always carry the Orange Otter, tied either on a small double hook, or on a single hook with a twist or two of lead wire round the shank. It is usually a sheet anchor. Steel Blue, Williams' Favourite, Rough Olive, Waterhen Quill, Greenwell's Spider, Treacle Parkin, Snipe and Orange, Burton Blue, Silver Twist, Red Tag and many more are all good grayling flies.

When you wish to try the true nymph, fall back on that selection from Mrs Sawyer. You will not need a great range of patterns, and the ones you get from her should see you connected to some good grayling—once you have acquired the technique.

It may not be out of place here to impress upon the reader that practice in fishing is as necessary as it is in any other sport. Yet you meet men on the river bank either bad-tempered or depressed because they are having casting difficulties, or are slow on the strike or heavy-handed when playing a fish. What do they expect? After moaning for some time they tell you that they have not had the time to fish since last year, or in some cases, it is several years.

Can you imagine a golfer who did not practise? The great pro's consider that they are slipping if they don't play every day. As for good shots—they don't just happen. They may be men with a flair and a quick eye and a good swing, but they still have to keep in practice.

To quote Oliver Kite, 'I reckon to be out of practice if I go three days without fishing. If you can't get to a river, try the local canal, duckpond, swimming bath, or, failing all else, dry land, a lawn, garage, hangar or other open space. At least you can go through the motions and keep your wrist in trim. People who say they haven't time to practise are convincing only when they never go to bed.'

Chapter 8

Lake and Reservoir Fishing

THIS HEADING covers a wide range of waters. The large water supply reservoirs such as Blagdon and Chew come readily to mind, and these, and the other numerous reservoirs, have attracted great numbers of anglers from all stations in life. They appeal to the working man, particularly during the close season for coarse fish. Those who find themselves unable to rent river or brook fishing, either due to its shortage in days of great demand, or from lack of funds, fish the lakes and reservoirs—as do the wealthier anglers who find that salmon fishing is now being priced beyond their reach. The reservoirs also attract another class of angler; the man who fishes with his brains. The scientist, the entomologist, the enthusiastic amateur fly dresser, the engineer rod builder—in short, such observant and painstaking men as Richard Walker, T. C. Ivens, David Collyer, Geoffrey Bucknall, Thomas Clegg, John Goddard, and others.

As a result a new approach to still water fishing is presented to the angling public, who had hitherto been content, to some extent, to go on in the old way of presenting either a dry fly, which was comparatively simple, or a team of wet flies of well-known and orthodox description, at any depth under water that the buoyancy of the flies and the casting line dictated, irrespective of the depth at which the fish were likely to be feeding at that time of day or season.

When I say presented to the angling public I mean that they have had a bombardment of science, new fly dressings, and methods by which they could cast a fly long distances, or fish it either on the bottom, just above the bottom, midwater, or at any other depth and at any rate of speed required. Since the 1950s the angling press has not gone short of instructive articles in its journals, many of them excellent, and a number of first-class books have appeared.

But the fishing in these still waters is not confined to the great reservoirs. There are small lakes being developed all over the country, but particularly in the south, and new ones being constructed wherever an adequate supply of pure water is available; the so called 'put and take' fisheries where growth can be very rapid, and three-, four- and five-pound trout are no longer rarities. Less happily, in some such fisheries the subscription rates have almost caught up with the prices asked for moderate salmon water.

In addition to these there are the tarns of Wales, waters which produce small fish for the most part, and a considerable expenditure of energy to reach them. In many of these the fish rise, find out the deception and reject the fly long before your reactions catch up.

The large waters of Scotland and Ireland require special treatment again and many of these are not as easy as they are made out to be. The great lakes of Ireland, Conn, Mask and so on, have to be fished many times to gain experience of the weather conditions (some of which can be extremely dangerous), the times to fish, the methods and the flies. As a general rule they are boat-fished in the old style, with a rather longer than usual rod, tripping the droppers, and not getting down too deep. I have proved to my own satisfaction, however, that the modern English reservoir techniques can pay in these waters, when weather conditions are suitable.

And are there some big trout there! I shall not forget a rough day on Conn when the troughs between the unpleasantly high waves were revealing great rocks and ledges which we had not previously known existed. I was pretty scared because the bottom of the boat was more than half-rotten and one slap on a rock in those troughs would have been the end. Whilst I was gazing gloomily at the water, and attempting to fish a fly, a trout came out and skittered along the surface, just as small fry, in terror of their lives, come out in front of a hunting pike or perch. This poor fish wore a look of terror, and when I tell you that all this happened within three yards of my eyes and the trout was certainly heavier than ten pounds, you can let your imagination conjure up what kind of predator was in pursuit.

Anything could live in these great lakes and it is a matter of astonishment to me that John Garvin's 53 lb pike record has never been beaten.

Lake and reservoir fishing can be most interesting but we all have our different approaches to it. I get bored with too much of the same water and need constant change of scene to keep my interest alive. I well remember the comment of a friend with whom I shared a boat at Blagdon last year. It was evening, the lake was low and uninteresting, and the only hope seemed to be the last hour. As we sat off Home Bay point a dozen or more anglers took up their stations along Green Lawn. They did not hurry and it was not until the sun was down that they really went to work. And did they go to work! My friend said, 'Look at those tremendous casts. They are casting forty yards!' They were certainly getting it out, and they were stripping in pretty fast too. If a working party from a prison had been condemned to such hard labour, every do-gooder in the country would have been marching in protest! 'How can they call that sport?' said my friend, and I agreed with him most heartily.

My idea of fishing these waters is to wander off and fish the near weed beds, and gradually increase the length of my casts if necessary. It is productive, too. But the standard treatment seems to be to stab a landing net into the bed of the lake, give an aggressive glare round like a dog with a bone, and then proceed to cast the maximum distance at the first throw.

You do get freak hot spots. One such at Chew gave fourteen fish in an hour or so to two of us sharing a boat. It is always worth keeping an eye open for unusual features.

The main bones of contention in lake fishing arise in deciding how and when to use which fly out of the thousands available.

I found that excellent book by John Veniard *Reservoir and Lake Flies* most interesting and informative in every way, but the thing that struck me was that the Freeman's Fancy was the first fly to appear on the cover. This fly, when I used it first to such good effect, was suggested to me one day when I was fishing

Cofton with Courtney-Williams. He swore by it and on his recommendation I used it and found it extraordinarily effective. Oddly enough it was a little-known fly at that time—about forty years ago, and remained so for very many years. Particularly in the evening this fly, always fished in a small size, caught fish after fish and was quite unbeatable. So indeed was his father's fly—Williams' Favourite—but this fly did well in the daytime also. Now why is it that certain flies of such a fancy type are so good? It cannot be because they are used more, which is the usual argument. Prior to that occasion when Courtney recommended them I had always been very conservative in my choice of flies, using in all conditions Invicta, Claret and Mallard, and Butcher—and very consistently successful they were. I then substituted the Freeman's Fancy for one of the old favourites, and it always caught more fish. It is odd how certain flies prove winners for a certain period, or in certain hands. I have used this fly on occasions since but never with quite the same success. Can it all be faith? I suppose the same thing happened with the Wickham's. Once upon a time the infallible fly, but not all that popular nowadays.

It is no use my attempting to give a detailed instruction on which flies to use, at what depth, and how to catch the big trout when others cannot, for the very simple reason that it has all been done before so well, and so frequently, by fine anglers who have devoted to lake fishing as many hours as I have to salmon fishing and brook pottering. But, if you should be a bit confused by all the science, and the conflicting fly recommendations of the experts, perhaps a simple list may help you. I will just name a few flies that have done me good service, but remember my claims are modest. I have rarely caught my limit on a reservoir, and I cannot remember catching a brownie over 5 lb in weight.

Freeman's Fancy (always small, sizes 12–14), Alder, Invicta, Claret and Mallard, Butcher, Black Pennell, Black Lure, Connemara Black, Worm Fly, Watson's Fancy, Grenadier, Williams' Favourite, Teal and Black, and that great attractor, the Muddler Minnow. I have caught a few fish on the variants such as Black Muddler, and a fancy thing with a good deal of orange in it, but they do not compare with the original Muddler. On its day it is a fantastic killer, fished in all manner of ways. Floating, midwater, deep down, and pulled fast or slow, smoothly, or in jerks. Even on the seemingly hopeless days it usually collects a brace to save the day. I called this fly 'that great attractor' because I hesitated to describe it as a fly, but in fairness to it I suppose the floater could be taken for a sedge. Anyhow, it is a great killer, and it appeals to salmon, too. Never be without it.

Luck with flies is a funny thing! I have tried the Alexandra on and off for over fifty years and cannot remember ever catching a fish on it. And yet I suppose other anglers do.

For useful additions to your nymph box, when going lake fishing, do not forget Amber Nymph, Black Buzzer, Red Buzzer, Lake Olive Nymph, Pheasant Tail Nymph, Sawyer's Killer Bug, Corixa, in several sizes and Shrimps in various colours.

I have done well with all these flies, and can therefore recommend them. There are dozens more I have not mentioned as my aim is to keep the list limited. There are also others on which I have had quite a number of fish. Matukas are good, Dry Daddy Long Legs pick up a few fish, and so on, but you cannot carry them all or you will spend all your time changing flies instead of fishing.

When you read the excellent, and beautifully illustrated fly books which are available, you will realize that there is so much repetition and so much close similarity in these vast numbers of flies that they cannot possibly be justified, and you might agree that it is more profitable, in terms of fish caught, to concentrate on a few proven patterns.

Chapter 9

Fishing Fun

Has much of the fun gone out of fishing? Is humour being overshadowed by the much more serious problems of modern life, or am I reading the wrong books and journals? I don't know, but one thing seems certain, and it is that fishing is no longer enlivened by all the delightfully funny books and articles which were written to record the sporting adventures of the Edwardians.

Books dealing with the theory and mechanics of fishing are more numerous than ever, but lighter books are conspicuous by their absence. Perhaps laughter has gone out of fashion. Advances in tackle design and techniques make fishing a much easier and far less laborious sport than it used to be in the old days. Travel has been speeded up, and yet we don't seem to have sufficient time to laugh. But surely just as many humorous situations must arise from day to day. In this I may be wrong. Perhaps some of the fun departed with the over-running reel and the consequent bad language. Perhaps bulls are more gentlemanly in their behaviour, or fences sounder than they were, and the delightful spectacle of your friend searching frantically for an opening to let him out of a bull-infested field, has departed for ever. And, of course, the Edwardian really did have a lot more fun, and far less strain and tension. A man had time to laugh his way through a fishing day, and, more important, time to meditate and jot down his humorous experiences on his return home. Distractions such as wireless and television did not exist, and in Edwardian society when father dictated that the family should stay quiet whilst he reminisced, the family stayed quiet. It was a different world, in which nobody ever thought of increasing rents or behaving in a manner that suggested the precedence of money over sport. It is different nowadays. Only recently a small club of my acquaintance, with a bit of very poor salmon fishing and lots of coarse fish, had its rent increased ten-fold, due to the bidding of another fishing association. While all anglers welcome the increasing popularity of their sport, things like that do, perhaps, make it rather difficult to see the funny side of fishing. The members, when I met them, seemed to lack that twinkle of the eye that used to indicate their happy frame of mind!

Nevertheless, it would be refreshing to find a modern Sheringham, or for another G. E. M. Skues to appear. Apart from Skues' great knowledge and powers of observation, is anything more delightful than an evening browsing over *Side-Lines, Side-Lights and Reflections?*

Only recently an old friend came to spend a day or two with me. What did we remember? Certainly not the big fish nor the big days. They were there, somewhere, recorded in our diaries, but they were not important. If the workings of our minds and memories meant anything at all, it was that the humour and companionship of fishing meant far more than the actual catching of fish. A memory that made us laugh as much as any other, concerned a very beautiful spring salmon which we saw lying dead in one of the lesser-frequented pools of the Welsh Dee. It was March and numbers of fresh fish were running. I gaffed it out and was unable to find any cause of death. It had certainly not been hooked and lost. Our inquest showed a difference of opinion: he thought poison, and I thought concussion, as it was not an unheard-of thing in that locality for a pool to be bombed. We took the fish to our hotel, and, may the gods forgive us, tried to sell it to the proprietor. The holiday was almost over and he would not buy, so we took it home. It had been a failure as a fishing trip, so a bit of salmon was welcome. I took half and he took the remainder, and I did not see him for another week. When I did I was shocked to find a changed man with a haunted expression. By the time he had arrived home he had convinced himself that poison was the cause of death, but being a thrifty soul he did not want to waste anything. He also thought that there was just a faint possibility that my concussion theory was the correct one, and so he tried the fish out on the local butcher. He cut a few pounds and left it with his compliments. He lay awake that night and wondered if the butcher would be poisoned. To his temporary relief he found everything normal when he passed the shop next morning. A jolly-looking butcher bid him good-morning and said he was eating the salmon for dinner. He worried all day and could not settle to his work and he slept fitfully at night. On the following day he was horrified to find the butcher absent from his shop, and he dared not enter to find out the reason. But he came home early and returned to have another look before the shop closed. Perhaps he was worrying unduly and the butcher had merely been absent on some other business! But no. The assistant was in charge, and another sleepless night followed. And so it went on for five days until my friend was a mere shadow of his former self. In the meanwhile I had been fishing again and I called to give him some trout. My assurance that I had eaten my share of the fish and found it excellent did something to reassure him, but I could not finally remove his fears, so, on some pretext, I visited the shop myself and asked for the proprietor.

'I'm sorry sir,' I was informed, 'he is away fishing. He was given some salmon last week and it was so delicious he decided to try to catch one himself.'

I could see my friend's health returning as we laughed.

A little later on I went to visit another old friend in a nursing home. We laughed so much over one incident that I was nearly asked to leave. The sister feared for his stitches!

It was this way. He was the lessee of two fabulous fishing lakes. The great numbers of good pike and big perch we caught there had to be seen to be believed. This day was during the war, and aircraft from two nearby training grounds were overhead in numbers. We fished, regardless of the empty 20 mm ammunition cases ejected far overhead, which were plonking into the water all round our small boat. Suddenly a great bomber zoomed down to within a few feet of our heads and we thought we saw the front and rear gunners waving. On closer examination it was apparent that they were swinging their guns on to us. We laughed and said, 'Let the boys have their bit of fun, I expect they thought they would frighten us,' and by this time the plane was miles away. A few minutes later the same thing happened again. In fact, a lot of things happened together. The plane skimmed over us; I saw the big black crosses on the wings and fuselage, and at the same time a large pike took my spoon. I called out, 'Up with the weight, quick. It's a Jerry,' and in the middle of the confusion that followed, the pike ran hard in the opposite direction. We got up the weight, hitched the rope round a rowlock, and rowed for dry land as if all the fiends of hell were after us—as indeed they were. The outcome of it was that brute force worked, the pike succumbed to these shock tactics, and the plane came back shortly afterwards and bombed the dam. That, I think, was the liveliest bit of fishing I ever had. Needless to say, we took a rather poor view of it all at the time, but in retrospect—well, it didn't quite cause my friend to burst his sticthes, but we felt quite sure it was only because the quality of the surgeon's nylon was improving.

Chapter 10

Bass on Light Tackle.
Five years of sport off the Irish coast

MANY OF old Izaak Walton's exhortations to the novice angler have become out-dated: tackle improvements and speedy transport have seen to that. For the bass angler, however, one which remains as true as ever is the advice to be at the waterside at the very crack of dawn. For some this is an easy matter; for others it is very nearly impossible. I do not find it easy, and the whole day becomes unbalanced. But in one respect I am lucky. I can set myself to wake at any given time, which earns the gratitude of others sleeping nearby who hate the merry tinkle of an alarm clock at 4 o'clock, particularly in Ireland, where the hours before midnight are more often devoted to drinking than dreaming.

In periods of fair weather and when the tides are right, an hour before the first streak of grey in the sky is the time for action; shaving, hot tea, a bite of food and away. From my house to the little so-called harbour was a matter of minutes, but getting the boat and out-board motor ship-shape always took a little time. It is essential to be over the best fishing grounds near to the reef by the time the spring tide loses its full power and slackens sufficiently for an angler to fish. These 'springs' at their height are so powerful that boat management is difficult, and fishing is a virtual impossibility. When the slackening of the tide coincides with the first light of dawn it can be a period of fantastic fishing, if other conditions are right. That is the time to be, of all the places in the world, in the area of Carrick Point–Splaugh Rock and southwards, down-tide, past the little harbour and ancient church ruins of St Helens, off Co. Wexford.

So let us go fishing, as I did on many fair mornings during a five-year residence in Ireland. A local fisherman used to tell me that the fishing was nowhere near as good as it was in his boyhood, when the area was 'as stuffed with hungry bass as I was with Powers Whiskey after Paddy Doyle's wake'! That may be true, but they were still marvellous mornings, and I doubt if catches are as good today.

Wind is the important factor when deciding on a journey across these exposed waters. The 18–20 ft cots are flat-bottomed clinker-built boats with centre boards. Good sea boats but prone to 'slapping' in certain wave conditions. The flat bottom is an ancient idea for getting a boat ashore safely by means of wooden rollers, a hard but necessary operation when harbours are infrequent.

The first thing an angler/boatman does before leaving home is to study the trees. A slight ruffle in the leaves is acceptable although a dead calm is to be preferred, but if the wind is really moving the branches briskly it is fair to assume that the sea will be lively. Even this is safe enough always providing the direction is not against the tide. Strong wind against strong spring tide means discomfort and possibly danger. As light begins to break and you see little white horses far out, innocent though they appear, you may be sure that they are of uncomfortable size for a cot when you get out there. Caution is the keyword. We have all taken risks and most of us have got away with it, but if you have passengers aboard it is your responsibility to play safe.

On the morning I have selected at random from my records the sea was calm following a long period of sunny settled weather. The air and water temperatures were favourable to surface fishing for bass and expectations ran high. There is a sense of magic in the air that must stir the soul of even the most prosaic angler, and a world of space, solitude and peace is entered. The tide is still running strongly and the lobster-pot floats are under heavy strain and in many cases submerged. This is as it should be; you must be south of the reef known as Splaugh Rock when the tide slackens and the world begins to light up. At first you drift, then start the motor and search the area hopefully, waiting for signs of awakening life, and it is not long before the colour begins to show in the sky and with it a few advance scouts, the pathfinders of the gull tribe, glide overhead in a seemingly casual manner. But they are not as sleepy as they appear to be, drifting effortlessly on motionless wings and, no doubt, with the pangs of hunger adding keenness to their search. Suddenly it is 'action stations'. The first flurry of panic—stricken fry break the surface to escape fierce attacks made upon them by a shoal of bass, rising from beneath. And then the angler observes one of the miracles of nature! By some mysterious means the word is transmitted to the myriads of birds perched on the roosting rocks far away, and within minutes the air is full of clamour and diving and twisting hunters, bent on satisfying their hunger, and the battle for existence.

You are now within casting distance, but many of the birds have settled on the sea as the first attack seems to have subsided. Maybe the fry have gone deeper, but it is only a matter of time before the bass drive them up again. The gulls are waiting, as you are, for the next eruption which may be near to the boat or possibly several hundred yards distant.

Whilst the lull continues, a word about tackle. A 9 ft fibre-glass spinning rod, with a light easy butt action; a 5000 or 6000 ABU multiplying reel loaded with 12 lb line, or if you prefer it, a fixed-spool reel with an open face which you can check by finger pressure on the rim when a fish runs an unexpectedly long way, or a closed-face reel of the ABUmatic type. The latter is to be preferred for overhead casting, as there is no bale arm to swing round and pick up at the wrong moment, and if you fish two or three to a boat the overhead is the safer cast.

The best bait of all in my experience is the French plastic jointed Sand Eel, made in three sizes. These became difficult to obtain but no doubt, now that trade with France is made easier, they will appear again on the market. The large size for use when there is a good wave and in rather dull and windy conditions. It is a splendid heavy caster, and yet does not fish too deep. The medium size for quieter conditions and more sunshine, in clear water, and the small one for very bright clear flat calms.

I find that these baits beat all others. On numerous occasions, when a check has been made, they have resulted in bags three or four times heavier than those produced by other baits—the well-loved and time-tested German Sprat included.

I always break into my line about twelve inches above the bait and fasten a ball-bearing swivel by means of two 4-turn half blood-knots!

Never forget that the word 'bait' is the most important word in fishing. It is the only part of your expensive outfit that interests the fish. Your £20 rod and £18 reel are the means by which you deliver the bait: nothing else! So don't save money on baits. It is the surest road to disappointment. A bait that looks and works well is more than half the battle.

Before this digression the birds were riding the waves. Waiting for further action from below. Now it comes! Suddenly a considerable area of the sea becomes a turmoil of ravening bass, diving birds, and leaping, panic-stricken fry. The excitement and greed of the hunters is almost beyond belief. The whole area of activity usually moves down tide, so the outboard is throttled down as much as possible to minimise vibration. Don't forget that much of the time you are fishing over rocks which magnify such unnatural sounds. Keep about twenty-five yards away from the edge of the shoal of striking bass. The water will probably begin clear and the more stealthy the approach the better.

Out goes the bait, forty or fifty yards, and it is allowed to sink a little, for very often the really large fish are lying deeper. A fast retrieve and, with luck, you will be into your first fish of the day. Anything from 2 lb to 10 lb. They are great, really great, fighters. They very rarely jump, but fight a hard deep battle and are game to the last. In all probability a dozen or more fish will follow the hooked fish in. There is no more magnificent sight than a good 7 lb bass, with his entire armoury fully extended, fins erect, and refusing to admit defeat, being drawn towards the waiting net or small gaff.

The feeding pattern changes from day to day. On a good day you may follow the fish as they feed down-tide for half-a-mile; on others only for a hundred yards or so. Fish may take for a couple of hours, and only go off when there is a difference in the tidal flow, and the birds may lift suddenly and fly back up-tide to the scene of a fresh shoal's feeding activity, in which case it may be advisable to start up the outboard and begin casting to the new shoal. They may be keener, and the old shoal may be nearing satiation. Whichever mood is ruling on the day, keep hammering away and don't waste time. They might go off at any moment.

What may you expect to catch? That depends on many factors, piscine and human. I have taken over sixty good fish on a tide, but that was before it had been realised that the supply of bass, a slow-growing fish, was not inexhaustible. Today I limit my catch to my immediate needs and never kill a fish under three pounds. Returning bass is not the easiest of jobs. They are a mass of prickles and a stout left-hand glove and an efficient disgorger are essential for doing the job without inflicting damage to the fish.

On the days when fish are shy, or few in number on the surface, they may be feeding deep down. We will discuss this later. Sometimes a change of bait can do the trick. My favourite 'second bests' after the plastic Sand Eel, are Heddon River Runt plugs, ABU. Krill, Koster, Toby, Glimmy, Mepps and the Red Gill.

On occasions I have had fish on a tube fly with silver body and grey squirrel hackle. About 1/0 in size, which looks much like a fry. To catch a good bass on a trout fly rod is a most thrilling and enjoyable experience, but of course it takes longer to subdue a hard-fighting fish on such gear. I have found a light but strong fibre-glass rod (9ft, with a No. 9 floating line with sink-tip) is about right for this work. I have used much lighter rods including the Hardy Jets designed for 5 and 6 lines, but one really needs a pretty stout rod for this very hard and testing work.

When, as invariably happens at certain times of the day, the bass leave the surface and the surfeited birds fly off, heavy-laden, to their favourite siesta rocks, the fish occasionally continue feeding on, or just above, the sea-bed. When this happens it is always worth while going down deep with a really heavy bait, and doing a little sink-and-draw fishing. Although we have used this method for a long time it is only recently that it has acquired a status of its own. It is now known as pirk fishing and is a deadly method for bass, cod and pollock. Again, the conditions govern the type and colour of bait to be used, but a very dull brass or copper pirk has always been remarkably successful. Bright nickel is best for conditions of dirty water and when the sediments have been stirred up by heavy seas. Another interesting fact is that

I have often found that the average weight of fish caught in this way has been a lot higher than when surface fishing. The method is simple. Lower the bait and hit the bottom with a good bump that will stir up whatever the particular type of sediment is; raise the rod some three or four feet and then let the bait go down hard again. On innumerable occasions the average size of fish in the bag on sand-eel has been 4½ lb. On deep pirk, over 7 lb! Needless to say, and as many fresh water anglers will have discovered for themselves, the same method, with smaller baits, can be deadly for pike, chub and perch. In fresh water a few salmon, thinking themselves well and safely established in deep and rocky holes where the spinner and fly pass them by on a higher plane, have made their final mistake in this manner.

I cannot say very much about natural bait fishing for bass. Sand eels, prawns, and many other such-like creatures are deadly, but they are an appalling nuisance to collect and keep alive—and I have an intense dislike of the secondary sport of wallowing in sea pools with a little net and aching back, trying to catch the elusive little wretches. One easy-to-get and very deadly bait is a small mackerel fished between the rocks and ledges. The big boys are very partial to these.

In Ireland the most popular bait is the German Sprat. It is used so generally and frequently that it has, no doubt, accounted for a greater total weight of fish—bass, mackerel, and pollock—than any other. It is cheap, easy to cast, and obtainable everywhere. But that does not mean to say it is the best. The Sand Eel is a far more killing bait and has enabled me to kill more fish to my own rod than boats containing two or three anglers fishing hard. The Sprat is showy and when an unsophisticated shoal of bass first encounter it they take it well, but brighter days and crystal-clear waters of summer make the fish shy of it after a time. The less showy and more natural Sand Eel does not lose its attraction in the same way, and if fish should pluck at the large size instead of taking it properly, they will almost certainly take the smaller ones with greater confidence.

Before it was revealed by the press, reporting the findings of scientific bodies, that the supply of bass is not unlimited and that their growth rate is terribly slow, many anglers, especially in Ireland, were unthinkingly guilty of taking too many. Vast shoals were seen on the surface, feeding over large areas, and it was assumed that the supply was inexhaustible. Now that the true facts have been revealed the majority of right-thinking bass fishermen have adopted a more reasonable attitude and self-imposed restrictions are the rule rather than the exception. A start towards sanity has been made in Ireland where a size limit, albeit an absurdly low one, has become law. It is just about time that this country came to its senses and took a good hard look at sea fishing limits, and fishery conservation as a whole. Foreigners are still fishing close inshore and tearing up the spawning beds; estuary nets, in low water conditions when rivers are suffering from drought, are slaughtering vast numbers of salmon and other fish. 'Hereditary rights' and the 'poor netsman's living' are the standard excuses. Nonsense!

As in most other directions, money, and the greed for it, lies at the bottom of the matter. Bass are in great demand, being particularly popular delicacies in France and Germany. The present price, a very high one, encourages the commercial and semi-professional fisherman to fish to excess, but in all these things there would not be a problem if there was not a receiver. Again, the answer is simple: ban exports! But I fear that the Government will take some convincing.

Quite apart from the Japanese nylon nets, invisible to fish, inexpensive and easy to get, which should be subject to very severe laws, one of the worst offenders in devastating the shoals of small school bass, is the man or boy who spends his evening on the sea wall, fishing lug or ragworm and catching dozens and dozens of tiny 9 in. to 12 in. bass. I have seen cases and cases of these immature innocents being packed in wholesalers' yards in Ireland ready for flying—flying, mark you, regardless of expense—abroad.

The angler visiting Ireland is unlikely to have his own boat and outboard. He would be wise before the event to make a close scrutiny of the craft to which he is entrusting his life, for many small boats in that delightful country are in a poor state of repair. Indeed, the boats in some English ports are not much to write home about, so look the boat over carefully before you take the plunge! You will know a sea-worthy boat when you see one and recognise a skipper who is workmanlike and tidy. Such qualities are very apparent if you have an eye for them. Some boats are beyond description. Outboards tied up with copper wire and insulating tape; anchors attached to four or five fathoms of worn-out rope for use when the sea-bed may lie at six times that depth, and one oar with very little blade left on it. All this, and a scruffy boatman, sometimes none too sober, bundled untidily into a boat which shows obvious signs of damage patched over with pitch. Not a very good insurance risk!

When you have satisfied yourself about the skipper and the boat, your problems are not always over. A favourite Irish expression is 'When the good Lord made time he made plenty of it'. That just about sums up the whole philosophy. Time doesn't mean very much. You may arrange to be at the boat at nine o'clock in the morning, but the boatman will be quite unabashed when he turns up an hour later. An enquiry at his cottage usually meets with the same reply, 'Patrick is in the bed.' At other times your arrival at such an hour, as arranged, shows an empty harbour and an equally empty seascape. Enquiries will reveal that a party of old friends arrived and met up with 'your man' in the local. They then decided to go out at dawn but would not think of informing you. Waiting on the quay you will be driven to the verge of insanity or suicide as they come merrily round the harbour wall to reveal a boat brimming over with glorious silver bass.

These are some of the difficulties associated with fishing the smaller and best fishing spots. They do not occur when you go to the larger, properly organised, resorts such as Kinsale where splendid boats and very knowledgeable skippers are available. Here you find a sheltered harbour, safe and well-found boats and good hotels.

Just one more warning to the holiday angler whose body is not attuned to hard work: to the man no longer in his youth, or lacking fitness and hard muscles due to a life spent very largely sitting in his office chair. He is inclined to think that once he is 'away from it all' he can do things that the local, who has been at the job since he was a boy, takes in his stride. There are many long and very 'fishy-looking' stretches of coast which lack harbours worth the name. The tantalising thing is that very often it is next to impossible to launch a boat to get afloat on these seas. The reason, I suppose, is that whilst these coasts with their reefs and dangerous rocks are very much favoured by bass and pollock, they are not much use to the commercial netsman. To get your own boat afloat, assuming you have one on a trailer behind your car, is very difficult and hard work. Light fibre-glass boats, inflatables, and marine ply creations are not too much of a problem to launch, but unfortunately they are not the ideal boats for such coasts. The traditional cots are sturdier but although the task of rolling them up and down the beaches is all very well for weight-lifters, it is beyond the strength of the average city dweller or professional man. I have seen two heart attacks result from this boat-heaving, and I can personally vouch for the damage it can do to the spinal region. I have suffered from slipped discs and strained ligaments and dislocated vertebrae, ever since I embarked on such stupidity. I have also learned that inflatable rollers are much easier things with which to work than the usual wooden ones.

This may all sound a rather perilous and inadvisable type of sport, but I think the answer is to get things organised and laid on properly before embarking on the actual fishing. One essential is a good and reliable contact man on the coast. Two would be better, if you can find them.

So many people new to angling (and some that aren't so new to it) think that once a few good books have been read and some rods, reels and baits purchased, they can dash off to the coast and catch fish. There is a bit more to it than that. A careful study is necessary. It is not very much use fishing for bass too early in the year before the shoals arrive. Temperature is the governing factor controlling that. One year will see the vast shoals of fry on the move in April. The next year may be cold, and the fry and the chain of predators following them will not arrive until June.

The best advisers are local anglers, publicans, and retired gentlemen who know how to use their eyes and brains. I prefer them to tackle dealers, hoteliers, and tourist and travel agents: they haven't any axe to grind! This was borne in on me very forcibly one day when I was painting my boat at St Helens in Co. Wexford. A very sad and depressed man came up to me and asked my advice. He lived in Cambridge and had brought his two sons over to enjoy some of the fabulous bass fishing cracked up by the Tourist Board. They had been wandering about for ten days trying to cast from the beach, and failing to get a boat anywhere. Their holiday money, over £100, had nearly gone, and they had not caught a single fish of any description. 'What made you come in April?' I asked. 'The advertisements,' he said. 'They said the fish were there to catch at every cast; specimen fish,'—or words to that effect. They did not say anything about season, or 'don't come too early, or too late'. I sympathised with the poor fellow. I had met many like him who had been misled by advertisements that were attractive: too attractive!—and had swallowed them without making very thorough enquiries. In fact, in my early days I have been caught in the same way.

I have not so far written very much about the actual catching of fish. Accounts of past days, and the size and number of fish caught soon begin to pall on the reader. In certain directions, such as outsized fish and exceptionally heavy bags, there may be something to be learned; but apart from the accusation of boastfulness, a lot of detailed past glories can only be a bore.

Generally speaking, whether in salt or fresh water the fisherman gets comparatively few red letter days. At the present time very large catches are controlled by the imposition of limits by most still-water trout fisheries. Salmon are having more than their share of misfortunes and the man who makes a pig of himself is not very popular, and bass are fewer than they were even seven or eight years ago. This paucity is in itself inflicting a control by discouraging anglers to the point where they just do not find it worth while to fish. All fish seem to have good years and lean ones, and it may be that bass have just had a number of bad seasons, but they have certainly been hammered since bass fishing was extolled by articles in every fishing magazine year in and year out. The writers who whip up all this enthusiasm to the masses, so that both coarse anglers and game fishermen turn to the sea in time of fresh-water close seasons, cannot grumble at the decline in sport. Everyone of us who has written a book or an article on the subject must bear his share of blame.

Fish are not always there for the taking, and many a time the bass fisherman goes out and has to chase the few odd feeding gulls and terns mile after mile. Every time it looks hopeful and you catch up with a bunch of them who are interested in something below, they take off again, and do the same thing a few hundred yards farther away. I have chased them from the coast right out to Tuskar rock, some seven miles, and then it has not turned into a good rise of fry and bass. Often the hunt for bass has been abandoned and a little good sport has been had by mackerel fishing. When the mackerel are on the top it is simple enough to tempt them with a lake-type lure on a fly rod or with a Mepps on a little 7 in. single-handed spinning rod and an ABU 505 reel. 5 lb b.s. line is heavy enough. When they are not on top they may be found with the same light gear a few fathoms down. Either the Mepps with the addition of a little lead, or a small nickel-plated pirk will do the trick. And do they fight! Every bit as game as a trout, and often far more active.

When the tide is running strongly and your boat is drifting at roughly the same speed you are on fair terms with a hard-fighting fish because you are all travelling together, but from an anchored boat the task would be almost impossible on fine tackle.

Conditions really look hopeful when small knots of terns begin to work. They may be of several species. Terns working usually indicate bass underneath them, but gannets and gulls are more likely to mean mackerel or pollock. There are few more delightful scenes on earth than a band of these perfect little sea-swallows hovering on fairy wings at one moment, and dipping to sip fry or sand-eels from the surface. Their beauty and delicacy is enchanting. Terns do not always have everything their own way. When the feeding has been good and they are well filled with the teeming fry, it is not uncommon for one or two skuas to appear on the scene. These birds look the robbers that they are; very relentless fliers, dark and persistent. They concentrate on one particular tern and all the twisting and turning of that agile flier cannot shake off the pursuit. It goes on in an amazing display of aerobatics; a mad dance almost as eccentric as peewits tumbling in the sky, but with more purpose. In the end the tern disgorges the contents of its stomach and then the chase is over. The skua settles down on the waves and consumes the fruits of its banditry.

The angler should always have an eye open for the beauty of birds. When the terns are busy elsewhere, there are usually a few gannets to watch. What superb exhibitions of high diving they give. That plummet into the waves with closed wings never seems to fail in its purpose.

Bass fishing prospects can never be calculated with any degree of certainty. Because you had a wonderful day yesterday, and as far as you can see conditions are identical today, it is by no means certain that they are. The barometer, the sea, the wind, sky, and state of tide may be almost the same but the second day turns out to be a total failure. This uncertainty, annoying as it may be at the time, is the element that keeps us keen and anxious to put it to the test. If you haven't read the splendid books of that genius G. E. M. Skues you should do so without delay. Particularly the sad story of Mr Castwell. He went to hell and was condemned to stand in one particular spot on the banks of a glorious trout stream. At every cast a two-pounder, in superb condition, took his fly and was duly netted by the ghillie. After a while he wished to desist, but that was not permitted. He must catch two-pounders, one after the other, throughout Eternity—HELL!

We could all enjoy a bit of this kind of hell occasionally, but there is no doubt that too much success can become tedious.

Although trailing a bait behind a boat cannot be classified as a particularly skilful or intelligent form of angling it is an odd fact that there are days, or parts of days, when a fish will follow a trailed bait for very long distances before it is able to make up its mind to swallow it—maybe the cause is any one of a dozen reasons. The most likely is that it is just after a period of heavy feeding, when the fish are almost satiated, or perhaps when they have been completely glutted and off feeding for some time, and they are just beginning to get the feeding urge again. It might be any one of many reasons, but I cannot quite believe that it is solely due to suspicion. The bait is some sixty to seventy yards away from the boat and the tackle is fine.

I have had very many days when, after a brisk morning's sport, fish have gone off completely. Even sinking pirks and trying all the dodges of fluttering and tumbling them near the sea bed has not produced a single extra fish. Then, as a last resort I have started up the motor, put out a long line—the Irish boatman insists on seventy yards—with a French Sand Eel at the end that matters. The only skill or artistry in this form of sport is possibly the way you manoeuvre your boat so that the bait skirts the rocks and reef in an attractive manner. The fact remains that I have often had five or six fish of well above the average size, and many of them have visibly followed the bait for considerable distances. In calm conditions they can be seen following the lure quite clearly, even though seventy yards away, because they furrow the water just behind the bait by poking out their noses now and again as if they are unable to make up their minds. On no account must the angler do anything at this stage. In all probability the fish will take firmly in due course. I fancy that I had the best results when trailing across the tide.

Lobster-pots and their lines are the great pest in this form of fishing. How I have cursed them! They always seem to be set in the most awkward spots and on one occasion I was over half-an-hour unravelling a great bunch of knitting with a 7 lb bass in the middle of it with one hand, whilst I endeavoured to control the cot and outboard, in a very strong tidal stream, with the other. But I got him in the end.

Chapter 11

Strange Tales
—Quite Possibly Almost True!

Odd stories, and equally odd happenings, are always cropping up in Ireland. The Irish philosophy can be summed up in the previously quoted favourite saying of the old timers, the 'lookers out to sea', the 'bridge leaners', and the weather prophets: 'When the good Lord made time, he made plenty of it'. There is a lot to be said for it, always providing you have not got a job to do, or you are not in a great hurry to catch the best part of the tide.

It certainly has compensations, too. For instance, one day I felt lazy and lapsed into this plenty-of-time mood. I sat under a stone wall looking at a featureless bit of country, and my laziness was almost immediately rewarded. By some ruins only a hundred yards away my glasses picked out a bird I had always wanted to see, and in forty years of bird-watching had never met with. There as large as life, were four hoopoes, and, to make a day of it, I saw two more on my way home.

On numerous occasions my reward has been the sight of killer whales, and many rare birds and fishes. One spell of idleness could have cost me dear! A number, quite a number, of very large basking sharks had settled in the bay, presumably to bask, for I never saw them do anything else.

I had decided to go fishing and took in my boat a very good fisherman and a small boy. We fished, and fortune did not smile on us, so we returned and dallied close to the rocks. Here we dozed, in fact I think we slept, whilst the small boy tried conclusions with the tiny pollock. Something prompted me to wake and I was interested to see the small boy about to make a thrust with my big shark gaff. 'Hi!' I cried. 'What are you doing?'—and that, fortunately, stopped him. I looked to port, where he was performing, and saw that we had drifted against a vast hulk. In fact we were touching it; a shark of some twenty or thirty feet. Probably the gaff would not have penetrated the blubber, but it just *might* have tickled the monster with disastrous consequences. Baskers are peaceful if left alone, but a scared one could slap its tail down on to a small boat with shattering consequences. Incidentally this same little boy covered himself with glory on the following day by hooking an 8½ lb bass on feathers. In the photograph I took afterwards, the fish was very nearly as long as the boy.

And whilst writing about really big fish there is the story of the king-size monster, told to me by an Irish fisherman friend whose word I respect. I had been telling him of a number of killer whales I had seen recently. They were hunting on the seaward side of Tuskar Lighthouse. 'Have you ever been really close to one?' I asked him. It did not take him long to think. 'I had an experience that I am never likely to forget,' he said. 'It was either a whale or some other monster as big as a whale, but I never want another like that one anywhere near to my boat again.'

'It was during the last war. You people were busy with the Germans and we were fishing day and night because the prices were high and money was easy to earn. It was a good period, too. Plenty of fish wherever you looked and the bay alive with bass. You never saw anything like it. There were also lots of German submarines about and we often saw them on the main shipping route past Tuskar, but they didn't take any notice of us. I had a good boat then, a 35-footer with a comfortable cabin and plenty of beam. A fine sea boat. She had a good engine and would go anywhere. We usually fished all night and this day we were homeward bound at about eight in the morning on a calm sea. Everything was peaceful and I had just had a bite of breakfast in the wheelhouse. As I walked out I thought I was seeing things. Just astern on the starboard side a great big black dorsal fin, or a tail, much larger I should say than a killer would have, rose up and up. I was so astonished and frightened that I don't really know what it was, because as fast as I could move I opened the throttle wide and closed my eyes for fear of what I might see next.

From what I can remember—and I hadn't touched a drop that week!—the last time I saw that awful black thing it was taller than our mast, and that was fourteen feet! It kept its distance and swam level with us. We were about three miles from this little harbour and there was just nothing I could do about it but go like hell, keeping my eyes ahead and with fear running down my spine as if I'd seen a ghost.'

'Did anybody else see this thing?' I asked—not exactly doubting the story, but wondering at the measurements.

'Yes, they did. Rory O'Connor saw it. But only for a second. I saw him come from below, because I must have shouted, and I knew he had looked astern and seen what I saw, because his face went from very red with sunburn to a dirty grey in a flash of time. It was only two days and four bottles of Powers Whiskey later that he recovered his proper colour. The fish left us after following for another five minutes.'

How true the story is I do not know, but it thrilled me at the time and made me wonder more than a little about going out in my 19 ft cot alone, but if you have read Gavin Maxwell's *Harpoon at a Venture* you would hesitate to doubt it. F. A. Mitchell-Hedges, in his *Battles with Giant Fish* refers to a Blue Whale of 82 ft stranded in the same bay on 25 March 1891.

You never know your luck with any fish. If you keep pegging away a blank period may turn into a richly rewarding one. This applies particularly to salmon fishing, for the travelling fish are here one moment and gone the next. But bass come and go, and they also come on the feed and go off again for no apparent reason. Even netsmen experience this, as the following story shows.

On the south-west coast there is a little cluster of cottages and a sea wall with a tiny harbour nestling behind it. A bit of fishing is done from the wall but results were far from sensational when I was there. Local anglers had seen large bass, but they were never caught, although soft crab, mackerel, rabbits' guts, razor fish, and most other baits had been offered. Every year a little old man, with a little old boat, and a trailer and motor car to which the same description could be applied, came for his annual holiday and a bit of fishing. He caught but little. This little man also tried his hand at trawling by dragging a small but serviceable bag net behind his boat, and in this he caught much seaweed and once some small pollock. In fact he was a bit of a joke—until one day! I was walking a mile or two to straighten out the kinks in my back caused by too much boat fishing, and as I rounded the end of the wall I stopped, literally frozen into immobility. Before me, on the concrete, lay the grandfathers of the bass tribe—five of them. The little man was as thunderstruck as I was. He said, 'And to think this should happen after all these years of catching nothing!' 'Did you get them in several hauls; were you at it all morning, or what?' 'No,' he said, 'they were all in the same haul, just as I was coming in.' 'Have you had them weighed,' I asked. 'Three times, by different men,' he replied. 'The five of them weigh 62 lb, and the largest is 13¾ lb.' They were coarse and not very attractive fish, dark in colour and with quite a different head from the silvery medium-sized bass caught more regularly. But it just shows that one day you may be lucky in spite of years of failure. But only if you persevere!

Index